Ireland U

Your Essential Trip Planner – Navigating the Emerald Isle's Culture, History, and Natural Beauty with Insider Tips for an Unforgettable Journey

Anita D. Brooks

Copyright © [2023] by [Anita D. Brooks]

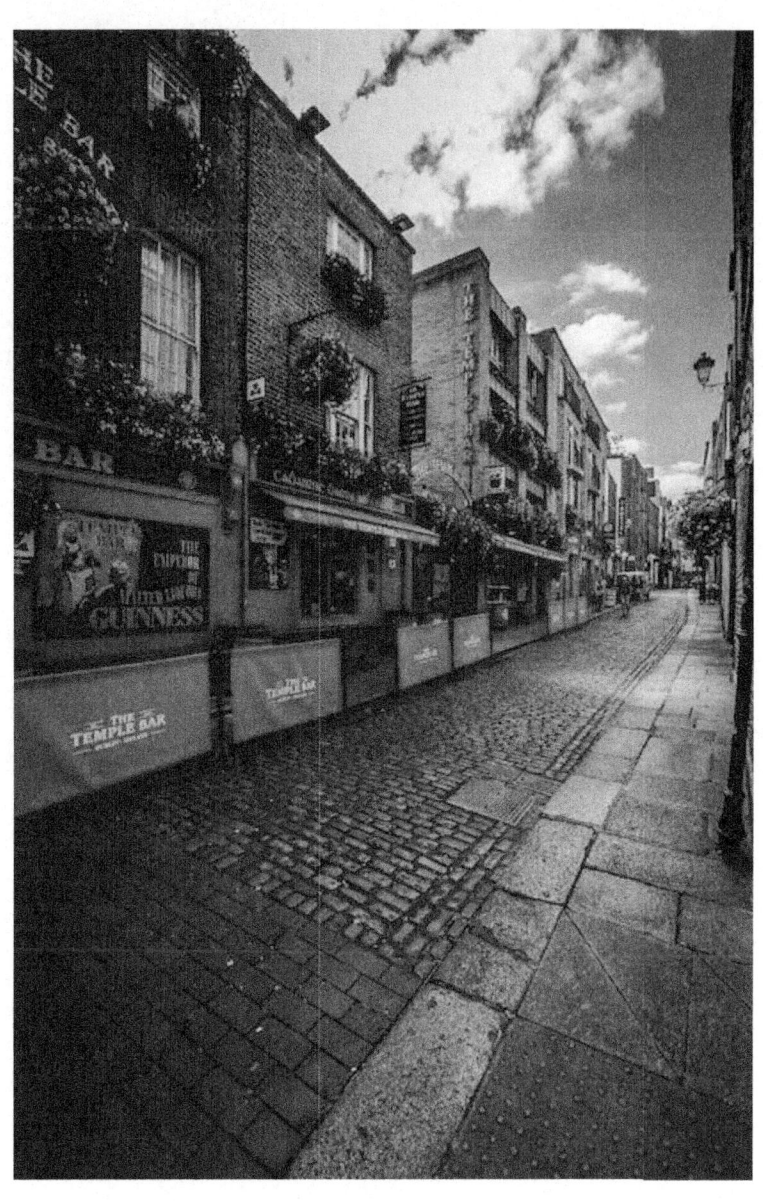

TABLE OF CONTENTS

Introduction to Ireland

A Brief Overview

Ireland, popularly referred to as the Emerald Isle, is a mesmerizing location that combines history, natural beauty, and dynamic culture seamlessly. Ireland is an island country that is located in the North Atlantic Ocean and is comprised of the Republic of Ireland and Northern Ireland. The following is a summary of the main reasons why Ireland is such an appealing tourism destination:

Rich History:

The history of Ireland is filled with stories of ancient civilizations, castles from the Middle Ages, and a turbulent past. Uncovering the mysteries of Ireland's history may be accomplished by visiting ancient locations such as the Rock of Cashel, Blarney Castle, and Newgrange Park.

The beauty of Ireland is a mosaic of rolling green hills, towering cliffs, and peaceful lakes. It is without a doubt one of the most breathtaking landscapes in the world.

Throughout the years, poets and authors have drawn inspiration from the natural grandeur that can be seen in places such as the Giant's Causeway, the Cliffs of Moher, and the famous Ring of Kerry.

Explore beautiful towns where it looks as though time has stopped moving and discover the charm of these places. You may take a walk through the medieval alleyways of Kilkenny, see the colorful homes of Kinsale, or enjoy the warmth of Dingle's traditional pubs.

Dynamic Cities:

Dublin, the nation's capital, is a city that is brimming with vitality and activity. Explore its ancient monuments, like as Trinity College and Dublin Castle, and absorb the bustling atmosphere of Temple Bar. Belfast in Northern Ireland provides a combination of modernism and history, including the Titanic Belfast Museum and the murals of the Falls Road.

Cultural Heritage:

Ireland's cultural richness is visible in its traditional music, dance, and literature. Attend a raucous pub session, experience the elegance of Irish dancing, and dig into the writings of literary giants like James Joyce and W.B. Yeats.

Warm Hospitality:

The Irish is famed for their kindness and hospitality. Engage in interactions with people, sample traditional meals, and feel the warmth of an Irish welcome wherever you go.

Festivals and Celebrations:

Ireland comes alive with festivals honoring everything from music and arts to literature and gastronomy. The St. Patrick's Day celebrations are world-famous, but the nation stages a variety of events throughout the year.

In essence, Ireland's attractiveness rests in its seamless combination of old charm and contemporary vibrancy, making it a must-visit destination for anyone seeking a memorable and culturally rich travel experience.

Why Visit Ireland

Ireland draws tourists with a unique combination of stunning scenery, rich history, and friendly friendliness. Here are strong reasons to make Ireland your next trip destination:

Scenic Landscapes: Ireland is a visual feast, with beautiful green scenery, craggy beaches, and calm lakes. From the renowned Cliffs of Moher to the gorgeous Ring of Kerry, the landscapes are both magnificent and unique.

Rich History and Heritage: Immerse yourself in Ireland's rich history, from ancient Celtic ruins to medieval castles. Explore the secrets of Newgrange, marvel at the ancient magnificence of Trim Castle, and uncover the legends inscribed into the stone walls of the Rock of Cashel.

Vibrant Cities: Dublin, Belfast, Galway - Ireland's cities are vibrant centers of culture, history, and modernity. Experience the exciting atmosphere of Dublin's Temple Bar, dig into Belfast's maritime heritage, and appreciate the bohemian charm of Galway.

Traditional Music and Dance: Let the soul-stirring strains of traditional Irish music and the rhythmic rhythms of dancing enchant you. Pubs around the nation come alive with boisterous sessions, delivering a genuine and full cultural experience.

Literary Legacy: Ireland possesses a rich literary legacy, with notable writers like James Joyce, W.B. Yeats, and Oscar Wilde. Visit Dublin's Trinity College to view the Book of Kells and follow in the footsteps of literary geniuses.

Warm Hospitality: The Irish are famous for their kindness and warmth. Experience true hospitality as you participate in talks with locals, drink a pint in a comfortable pub, and experience the feeling of community throughout your tour.

Culinary Delights: Indulge in the tastes of Irish cuisine, from substantial stews and fresh seafood to artisan cheeses and world-famous drinks. Sample traditional delicacies and experience the bustling culinary scene in towns and villages alike.

Festivals & Celebrations: Ireland knows how to rejoice. Attend exciting festivals like St. Patrick's Day, immerse yourself in music and cultural events, or join local festivities that exhibit the country's vivacious character.

Outdoor Adventures: Outdoor lovers will find their paradise in Ireland. Hike along seaside paths, go on picturesque drives, or try your hand at aquatic sports. The scenery inspires exploration and adventure.

Unforgettable Experiences: Ireland provides a tapestry of experiences - from kissing the Blarney Stone for eloquence to touring historic monastery ruins. Each day unfolds with fresh tales and unique interactions.

In essence, Ireland is a country that begs you to not simply visit but to become a part of its rich fabric, where every corner carries a tale, and every moment is a chance to make lifelong memories.

Best Time to Visit

Choosing the perfect time to visit Ireland depends on your choices and the sort of experience you desire. Here are the concerns for various seasons:

Spring (March to May):

a. **Blooming Landscapes:** Spring brings Ireland's landscapes to life with brilliant hues and beautiful flowers.

b. **Mild Weather:** Enjoy mild temperatures, making it ideal for outdoor activities.

c. **Fewer Tourists:** Spring is considered shoulder season, giving a calmer ambiance at major destinations.

Summer (June to August):

a. **Long Days:** Experience lengthy daylight hours, allowing for extensive exploring.

b. **Festivals & activities:** Summer includes several festivals, outdoor activities, and cultural festivities.

c. **Warmer Temperatures:** Enjoy somewhat warmer weather, while rain is still frequent.

d. **Peak Tourist Season:** Expect increased crowds, particularly in famous tourist areas.

Autumn (September to November):

a. **Foliage and Tranquility:** Witness the shifting hues of fall leaves in a more serene atmosphere.

b. **Mild temps:** Enjoy nice temps before the winter cold comes in.

c. **Cultural Events:** Experience numerous cultural events and festivals.

Winter (December to February):

a. **Festive Atmosphere:** Embrace the festive mood with Christmas markets and events in cities.

b. **Cozy Pubs:** Winter is an excellent time to enjoy the warmth of traditional Irish pubs.

c. **Fewer visitors:** Experience a peaceful Ireland with fewer visitors during the off-peak season.

d. **Colder Temperatures:** Be prepared for colder and wetter weather, with the risk of snow in certain locations.

Overall Considerations:

a. **Rainfall:** Ireland is notorious for its rain, so regardless of the season, it's important to wear waterproof gear.

b. **Temperate Climate:** Ireland has a temperate marine climate; therefore, excessive temperatures are unusual.

The ideal time to visit Ireland depends on your tastes and the sort of experience you seek. For pleasant weather and flowering scenery, spring is wonderful. Summer offers long days and a lively atmosphere, while autumn provides a more tranquil experience with changing foliage. Winter offers a joyous ambiance and fewer people, particularly in metropolitan areas. Ultimately, Ireland's charm is ever-present, and each season has its particular attraction.

Chapter One: Planning Your Trip

Entry Requirements

Passport: Ensure that your passport is valid for at least six months beyond your scheduled departure date.

Visa Requirements: Citizens from several countries, including the United States, European Union, Canada, Australia, and New Zealand, normally do not need a visa for short stays (up to 90 days). However, it's vital to examine the particular criteria depending on your nationality. Check the official website of the Irish Naturalisation and Immigration Service (INIS) for up-to-date information.

COVID-19 Guidelines: Given the worldwide circumstances, be updated about any special COVID-19 entrance procedures or travel restrictions. Check the latest instructions from the Irish government and the World Health Organization (WHO).

Travel Insurance: It is strongly suggested to have travel insurance that covers medical emergencies, trip cancellations, and unforeseen occurrences.

Proof of lodging and Return Ticket: Have proof of your lodging arrangements for at least the beginning portion of your trip. Additionally, it may be beneficial to have a return ticket or documentation of continuing travel.

Currency and Finances: Be prepared with appropriate finances for your stay. While credit cards are commonly accepted, keeping some local currency (Euro) in cash is advised for smaller enterprises or rural locations.

Customs Declaration: Familiarize yourself with Ireland's customs rules. Declare any objects that need to be declared upon admission.

Health Precautions: Ensure you are up-to-date on standard immunizations. Depending on your travel history, extra vaccines or health measures may be required. Check with your healthcare practitioner.

Driving in Ireland: If you intend to drive, verify whether your driver's license is valid in Ireland. Visitors from most countries may drive using their native driving license for up to 12 months.

Emergency Contact Information: Keep a record of emergency contact information, including the contact details of your country's embassy or consulate in Ireland.

Check for Updates: Before your departure, check for any updates or changes to entry criteria on official government websites.

Remember that entrance criteria might vary, so it's vital to keep informed and check the latest information closer to your trip date. Always go to the official government websites or contact the appropriate authorities for the most accurate and up-to-date information.

Currency and Money Matters

Currency: The official currency of Ireland is the Euro (€). Ensure you have extra cash on hand, particularly for little transactions or in locations where card payments may not be readily accepted.

Banking and ATMs: Ireland has a well-developed banking system. ATMs (Automatic Teller Machines) are extensively accessible in metropolitan regions and towns.

Use your debit or credit card to withdraw cash, and advise your bank of your trip dates to prevent any complications.

Credit Cards: Credit cards (Visa and MasterCard) are generally accepted in most locations, including hotels, restaurants, and shopping. American Express and Diners Club may not be as commonly utilized, thus it's essential to have a widely accepted card as a main method of payment.

Currency Exchange: Currency exchange services are accessible at airports, banks, and currency exchange offices in large cities. While credit cards are regularly used, keeping some local currency in cash might be beneficial, particularly in remote locations or for modest transactions.

Tipping: Tipping is traditional in Ireland. In restaurants, it's typical to leave a tip of roughly 10-15% if a service fee is not included. Tipping is also popular for taxi drivers, hotel workers, and tour guides.

Budgeting: Plan your budget including accommodation, food, transportation, activities, and mementos. Ireland may be somewhat costly, so having a clear budget helps control your costs.

Value Added Tax (VAT): Ireland has a Value Added Tax (VAT) on goods and services. Non-EU citizens may typically seek a refund on VAT for certain transactions. Keep your receipts and ask about the VAT return procedure when making large purchases.

Safety Precautions: Be careful while using ATMs, particularly in busy places. Keep a watch on your stuff and utilize recognized ATMs affiliated with banks.

Currency Conversion applications: Consider utilizing currency conversion applications to remain current on exchange rates and manage your costs properly.

Contact Your Bank: Inform your bank about your trip dates and destination to prevent any complications with using your cards overseas. Check for any international transaction fees that may apply.

Emergency monies: Keep a modest quantity of emergency monies in a separate, safe area, such as a money belt or concealed bag.

By keeping these money considerations in mind, you may handle your finances effectively throughout your stay in

Ireland. Always be informed of the local traditions and payment habits to have a hassle-free trip.

Transportation Options

Navigating Ireland is a lovely experience, with different transit alternatives allowing flexibility and ease. Here are the primary methods to move around:

Car Rental:

a. **Advantages:** Renting a vehicle provides you the opportunity to explore rural locations at your speed. Ireland's gorgeous scenery is best enjoyed via driving.

b. **Considerations:** Drive on the left side of the road. Roads may be small, and some rural regions may not have substantial public transit.

Public Transportation: Buses:

a. **Advantages:** Ireland has a large bus network linking cities, towns, and even isolated places.

b. **Considerations:** Timetables might change, therefore it's vital to plan your travel.

Trains:

    a. **Advantages:** Ireland's rail network links major cities, giving a pleasant and picturesque travel.

    b. **Considerations:** Train services may be restricted in certain remote locations.

Taxis: Taxis are frequently accessible in cities and towns. It's a practical choice for short trips or when you choose not to drive.

Riding: Ireland provides great riding routes, particularly in rural regions. Many communities have bike-sharing systems and bike rentals are available.

Domestic Flights: For longer distances, consider domestic flights, especially if you want to link between locations fast.

Ferries: If you want to visit islands or explore the coastal areas, ferries are available. Major ferry routes include connections between Ireland and the UK.

Tours & Guided Transportation: Joining guided tours or booking private transportation for specialized excursions is a simple method to visit places without the burden of traveling.

Walking: Many cities and towns are pedestrian-friendly, enabling you to explore historical landmarks, shops, and cafés at a leisurely pace.

Ride-sharing applications: Uber and other ride-sharing applications exist in several metropolitan areas, giving an alternative to conventional taxis.

Accessibility: Consider the accessibility of transit choices if you have unique mobility requirements. Many services cater to tourists with impairments.

Tips:

Check transportation timetables in advance, particularly for buses and trains.

Plan for additional travel time, since roads in rural regions, may be slower to maneuver.

Familiarize yourself with public transit payment options and any travel cards or passes available.

Whether you choose the freedom of a rental vehicle, the convenience of public transit, or a mix of alternatives, Ireland's well-connected network makes it simple to see the country's many landscapes and cultural riches.

Packing Tips

Weather-Appropriate Clothing:

   a. **Layers:** Ireland's weather may be unpredictable. Pack layers to cope with shifting temperatures.

   b. **Waterproof Jacket:** A good-quality waterproof jacket is needed for the odd rain shower.

Comfortable Footwear:

   a. **Waterproof Boots:** Especially if you intend on touring the countryside or trekking.

   b. **Comfortable Walking Shoes:** Ideal for urban exploration and extended treks.

Adapters and Chargers:

   a. **Power Adapter:** Ireland uses the Type G electrical outlet. Bring a compatible adaptor for your devices.

   b. **Chargers:** Ensure you have chargers for your phone, camera, and other electrical devices.

Travel Insurance and Important Documents:

   a. **Insurance:** Carry travel insurance that covers medical emergencies and unforeseen situations.

b. Documents: Pack your passport, trip itinerary, lodging information, and any applicable visas.

Backpack or Daypack:

Daypack: Useful for day excursions, transporting basics, and storing goods while exploring.

Universal Travel Essentials:

a. **Travel-sized toiletries:** To conserve room and comply with airline requirements.

b. **Travel Pillow and Blanket**: Handy for lengthy flights or road journeys.

c. **Reusable Water Bottle:** Stay hydrated while decreasing waste.

Outdoor Essentials:

a. **Sunscreen:** Even on overcast days, UV radiation may be powerful.

b. **Hat and Sunglasses:** Protect yourself from the sun, particularly if you intend to spend time outside.

Currency and Payment Methods:

a. **Cash:** Have some local money (Euro) for little transactions or establishments that may not take cards.

b. **Credit/Debit Cards:** Notify your bank of your trip dates to prevent any complications with card use.

Backpack Essentials:

a. **Camera:** Capture the gorgeous scenery and unforgettable experiences.

b. **Travel Guide/Map:** Stay focused and organize your activities.

c. **Snacks:** Keep energy levels up throughout your adventures.

Weather-Resistant Gear:

a. **Umbrella:** Compact and durable for unexpected rain showers.

b. **Waterproof Bag or Cover:** Protect gadgets and papers from rain.

Clothing Accessories:

   a. Scarves and Hats: Useful for both fashion and warmth.

   b. Gloves: Particularly if you're coming during the colder months.

Health and Safety Items:

   a. First Aid Kit: Basic supplies for minor accidents or diseases.

   b. Prescription Medications: Ensure you have enough supply for the length of your vacation.

Entertainment:

   a. Books, E-books, or E-readers: For leisure or lengthy travels.

   b. Travel Games or Gadgets: Entertainment for leisure times.

Travel Locks:

Locks: Secure your luggage and belongings, especially in shared accommodations.

Sustainable Choices:

   a. **Reusable Shopping Bag:** Useful for souvenirs and groceries.

   b. **Refillable Water Bottle:** Reduce single-use plastic waste.

Personal Comfort:

Sleep Mask and Earplugs: Ensure a good night's sleep, particularly if you're staying in various lodgings.

Remember to adapt your packing list depending on the particular activities you want to conduct and the time of year you'll be visiting. Packing effectively means you're prepared for the many experiences that Ireland has to offer.

Chapter Two: Dublin - Ireland's Vibrant Capital

Historical Sites

Dublin, with its rich history spanning centuries, is home to various historical landmarks that highlight the city's cultural legacy. Here are some must-visit historical attractions in Dublin:

Trinity College and the Book of Kells:

a. **Location:** College Green, Dublin 2

b. **Description:** Trinity College, established in 1592, is Ireland's oldest university. Explore the magnificent campus and don't miss the Library's Long Room. The centerpiece is the Book of Kells, an elaborately illuminated book from the 9th century.

Dublin Castle:

a. **Location:** Dame Street, Dublin 2

b. **Description:** Originally erected in the 13th century, Dublin Castle has played a significant part in Ireland's history. Visit the State Apartments, the

Chapel Royal, and the ancient undercroft for an insight into Ireland's history.

Kilmainham Gaol:

a. **Location:** Inchicore Road, Kilmainham, Dublin 8

b. **Description:** This old jail played a vital part in Irish history, housing political prisoners over different eras. Take a guided tour to learn about Ireland's battle for independence.

St. Patrick's Cathedral:

a. **Location:** St. Patrick's Close, Dublin 8

b. **Description:** Founded in 1191, St. Patrick's Cathedral is the biggest in Ireland. Admire the Gothic architecture, tour the interior, and learn about its links to Jonathan Swift, the author of "Gulliver's Travels."

Christ Church Cathedral:

a. **Location:** Christchurch Place, Dublin 8

b. **Description:** Dating back to the 11th century, Christ Church Cathedral is another prominent Dublin monument. Visit the medieval crypt, climb the tower for panoramic views, and study the rich history inside its walls.

Malahide Castle:

a. **Location:** Malahide, Co. Dublin

b. **Description:** Located just outside Dublin, Malahide Castle dates back to the 12th century. Explore the medieval chambers, gardens, and the huge estate around the castle. 7.

National Museum of Ireland - Archaeology:

a. **Location:** Kildare Street, Dublin 2

b. **Description:** Dive into Ireland's archaeological legacy at this museum, displaying objects from prehistoric ages to the Middle Ages, including the Ardagh Chalice and the Tara Brooch.

National Museum of Ireland - Decorative Arts and History:

a. **Location:** Collins Barracks, Benburb Street, Dublin 7

b. **Description:** Housed in a former military barracks, this museum highlights Ireland's social, economic, and military history. The displays feature ornamental arts, weapons, and things linked to current history.

These historical landmarks provide a compelling tour through Dublin's past, giving insights into the city's growth and its effect on Ireland's history and culture.

Museums and Galleries

Dublin features a dynamic cultural landscape with a range of museums and galleries that appeal to varied interests. Here are some important institutions to explore:

National Museum of Ireland – Archaeology:

a. **Location:** Kildare Street, Dublin 2

b. **Description:** Discover Ireland's rich archaeological legacy, including ancient gold items, Viking treasures, and the famed Ardagh Chalice.

National Gallery of Ireland:

a. **Location:** Merrion Square West, Dublin 2

b. **Description:** Home to an important collection of European art, the National Gallery exhibits works by notable painters like as Vermeer, Caravaggio, and Jack B. Yeats.

Dublin City Gallery the Hugh Lane:

a. **Location:** Charlemont House, Parnell Square North, Dublin 1

b. **Description:** Explore modern and contemporary art at The Hugh Lane, noted for its spectacular stained-glass window by Harry Clarke and the relocated studio of Francis Bacon.

Chester Beatty:

a. **Location:** Dublin Castle, Dublin 2

b. **Description:** The Chester Beatty Library holds a wide collection of manuscripts, rare books, and art from civilizations around the globe, spanning over 5,000 years.

Irish Museum of Modern Art (IMMA):

a. **Location:** Royal Hospital Kilmainham, Dublin 8

b. **Description:** Set in a historic edifice, IMMA highlights current and modern art via exhibitions, installations, and a magnificent sculpture garden.

Science Gallery Dublin:

a. **Location:** Pearse Street, Dublin 2

b. **Description:** A vibrant facility within Trinity College Dublin, the Science Gallery investigates the convergence of art and science, offering interactive and thought-provoking exhibitions.

National Museum of Ireland - Decorative Arts and History:

a. **Location:** Collins Barracks, Benburb Street, Dublin 7

b. **Description:** Housed in a former military barracks, this museum concentrates on decorative arts, fashion, furniture, and Ireland's social, economic, and military history.

The Little Museum of Dublin:

a. **Location:** 15 St Stephen's Green, Dublin 2

b. **Description:** A beautiful museum in a Georgian townhouse, The Little Museum of Dublin presents a selected collection of antiques, pictures, and memorabilia depicting Dublin's 20th-century history.

Dublin Writers Museum:

a. **Location:** 18 Parnell Square, Dublin 1

b. **Description:** Celebrate Ireland's literary legacy at the Dublin Authors Museum, with exhibitions on great Irish authors, including Yeats, Joyce, and Wilde.

The National Leprechaun Museum:

a. **Location:** Jervis Street, Dublin 1

b. **Description:** Delve into Irish folklore at this fascinating museum, where interactive displays and storytelling explore the tale of leprechauns and other mythological creatures.

These museums and galleries provide a varied variety of experiences, offering insight into Ireland's history, art, literature, and cultural identity. Whether you're interested in ancient antiques or modern art, Dublin offers something to attract every tourist.

Entertainment and Nightlife

Dublin's robust nightlife and entertainment scene make it a must-visit destination for anyone seeking dynamic experiences. From traditional Irish pubs to sophisticated entertainment establishments, the city provides a varied selection of possibilities. Here's a taste of Dublin's entertainment and nightlife:

Traditional Irish Pubs:

The Temple Bar:

    a. Location: Temple Bar, Dublin 2

    b. Description: One of Dublin's most renowned bars, famed for live music, traditional Irish sessions, and a bustling environment.

O Donoghue's:

    a. Location: 15 Merrion Row, Dublin 2

    b. Description: A historic bar with a rich musical legacy, O'Donoghue's is a terrific spot to listen to live Irish folk music.

Live Music Venues:

Whelan's:

    a. Location: 25 Wexford Street, Dublin 2

b. **Description:** A popular venue for live music, Whelan's showcases a mix of local and international bands in a friendly environment.

Vicar Street:

   a. **Location:** 58-59 Thomas Street, Dublin 8
   b. **Description:** A bigger facility with outstanding acoustics, Vicar Street accommodates concerts, comedy acts, and events.

Dublin's Literary Scene:

The Gaiety Theatre:

   a. **Location:** South King Street, Dublin 2
   b. **Description:** Dating back to 1871, The Gaiety Theatre showcases a range of entertainment, including musicals, dramas, and comedy acts.

The Abbey Theatre:

   a. **Location:** 26/27 Lower Abbey Street, Dublin 1
   b. **Description:** Ireland's national theatre, features both classic and modern plays.

Nightclubs and Late-Night Venues:

Copper Face Jacks:

    a. Location: 29-30 Harcourt Street, Dublin 2

    b. Description: A prominent nightclub with numerous levels and a broad music playlist, drawing a vibrant audience.

The Button Factory:

    a. Location: Curved Street, Temple Bar, Dublin 2

    b. Description: A multipurpose facility featuring live music, DJ nights, and club events.

Comedy Clubs:

The International Comedy Club:

    a. Location: 23 Wicklow Street, Dublin 2

    b. Description: Enjoy a night of laughing with stand-up comedy performers at this well-known comedy club.

River Liffey Cruises:

Liffey River Cruises:

    a. Location: Bachelor's Walk, Dublin

b. **Description:** Experience Dublin's cityscape from a fresh viewpoint with a picturesque boat down the River Liffey.

Late-Night Eateries:

Leo Burdock:

a. **Location:** 2 Werburgh Street, Christchurch, Dublin 8

b. **Description:** A historic fish and chips establishment that's excellent for a late-night snack after a night out.

Cultural Events and Festivals: Check for cultural events, festivals, and special events occurring during your stay. Dublin holds several festivals promoting literature, music, and arts throughout the year.

Dublin's entertainment and nightlife cater to varied preferences, guaranteeing that tourists can find the right experience, whether they're seeking traditional Irish music, live shows, or frenetic nightclubs.

Accommodation Options

Dublin provides a broad selection of housing alternatives to suit diverse interests and budgets. Here are suggestions across several categories:

Luxury Hotels:

The Shelbourne, Autograph Collection:

    a. **Location:** 27 St Stephen's Green, Dublin 2

    b. **Description:** A historic hotel with magnificent accommodations, situated near St. Stephen's Green. The hotel radiates sophistication and provides exquisite restaurants and a spa.

The Westbury Hotel:

    a. **Location:** Grafton Street, Dublin 2

    b. **Description:** Situated in the middle of the city, The Westbury is noted for its beautiful accommodations, great service, and a rooftop restaurant with panoramic views.

Boutique Hotels:

The Dean Dublin:

a. **Location:** 33 Harcourt Street, Dublin 2

b. **Description:** A fashionable boutique hotel offers distinctive, elegant rooms, a rooftop bar, and a strategic position among nightlife attractions.

The Dylan Hotel:

a. **Location:** Eastmoreland Place, Dublin 4

b. **Description:** A boutique hotel with a modern style, situated in a peaceful region along the Grand Canal. It provides magnificent accommodations and a gourmet restaurant.

Mid-Range Hotels:

The Morrison, a DoubleTree by Hilton Hotel:

a. **Location:** Ormond Quay Lower, Dublin 1

b. **Description:** A contemporary hotel beside the River Liffey, close to attractions like Temple Bar. Stylish rooms and a riverfront patio add to the attractiveness.

The Mont Clare Hotel:

a. **Location:** Merrion Square, Dublin 2

b. **Description:** Situated near Trinity College and Merrion Square, this hotel provides pleasant rooms with a traditional flavor.

Budget-Friendly Options:

Generator Hostel Dublin:

a. **Location:** Smithfield Square, Dublin 7

b. **Description:** A stylish hostel with a young vibe, providing both dormitory and private rooms. It's positioned among cultural sites and features a bustling bar.

The Times Hostel - College Street:

a. **Location:** College Street, Dublin 2

b. **Description:** A budget-friendly hostel in a central location, offering clean and pleasant rooms. It's near to Trinity College and Temple Bar.

Self-Catering Apartments:

Staycity Aparthotels Dublin Castle:

a. **Location:** Chancery Lane, Dublin 8

b. **Description:** Modern apartments with kitchen amenities, excellent for individuals who want a self-catering alternative. Close to Dublin Castle and Christ Church Cathedral.

Airbnb:

Description: Explore numerous apartments, residences, and unique lodgings with Airbnb. This option allows for discovering local communities and frequently offers more customized experiences.

Tips for Booking:

Book in Advance: Especially during high seasons or events, arranging accommodation in advance is important.

Check Reviews: Before booking, examine reviews on sites like TripAdvisor or Booking.com to verify the hotel fits your expectations.

Location Matters: Consider the location related to your intended activities to improve your stay.

Dublin's numerous lodging choices appeal to a variety of interests, whether you're seeking luxury, boutique charm, mid-range comfort, or budget-friendly alternatives.

Chapter Three: Galway - A Charming City on the West Coast

The Cliffs of Moher

The Cliffs of Moher, one of Ireland's most beautiful natural monuments, are situated along the western coast of Ireland in County Clare. While Galway is a lively city on the west coast, it is not exactly near the Cliffs of Moher. However, Galway acts as a popular starting place for those eager to experience this beautiful natural beauty.

Getting from Galway to the Cliffs of Moher:

Guided Tours:

a. **Advantages:** Many tour companies provide day tours from Galway to the Cliffs of Moher, offering transportation, a guide, and frequent stops at other spectacular sights.

b. **Considerations:** Check the length of the trip and whether it includes other sites, such as the Burren or Doolin.

Self-Drive:

a. **Advantages:** Renting a vehicle gives flexibility in your schedule and the option to explore adjacent locations at your speed.

b. **Considerations:** Ensure you are comfortable driving on Irish roads, and account for journey time, parking, and entrance to the Cliffs.

Public Transportation:

a. **Bus Services:** Regular bus connections link Galway to places around the Cliffs of Moher, such as Doolin or Ennis. From these towns, you can arrange local transportation to the cliffs.

b. **Considerations:** Public transit may have set timetables, so plan appropriately.

Exploring the Cliffs of Moher:

Visitor Center:

a. **Description:** The Cliffs of Moher Visitor Experience includes information, exhibitions, and amenities. It's a wonderful starting place for your visit.

b. Activities: Explore the interactive exhibits, enjoy refreshments, and acquire data about walking routes.

Coastal Walks:

a. **Description:** Enjoy picturesque walks along designated trails that give diverse viewpoints of the cliffs and shoreline.

b. **Recommendation:** The Cliffs of Moher Coastal Walk from Doolin to Hags Head affords amazing vistas.

O'Brien's Tower:

a. **Description:** O'Brien's Tower, positioned at the highest point of the cliffs, provides panoramic views. It's a historic monument with a long history.

b. **Tip:** Climb to the peak for magnificent panoramas of the surrounding region.

Boat Tours:

a. **Description:** Some companies provide boat cruises leaving from adjacent towns like Doolin. These boat cruises give unique views of the cliffs from the water.

b. **Advantages:** Experience the cliffs from a fresh viewpoint and, at times, meet local animals.

Tips for the Visit:

Weather Conditions: The weather on the West Coast may be varied, so dress in layers and pack waterproof gear.

comfy Footwear: Wear strong and comfy shoes, particularly if wanting to explore walking pathways.

Visitor Safety: Adhere to safety guidelines and stay within designated areas. The cliffs contain tremendous fall, and vigilance is necessary.

Whether you select a guided tour, self-drive adventure, or public transportation, seeing the Cliffs of Moher from Galway guarantees a remarkable experience of Ireland's spectacular natural beauty.

Connemara National Park

Nestled in the west of Ireland, Connemara National Park is a treasure of natural beauty, featuring a rough environment, various ecosystems, and outdoor activities. Here's a guide to explore Connemara National Park:

Location: Letterfrack, County Galway

Description: Connemara National Park is located in the heart of Connemara, comprising approximately 2,000 hectares of magnificent mountains, bogs, heaths, and forests.

Diamond Hill: Diamond Hill is the showpiece of Connemara National Park. The well-marked pathways lead to the peak, affording panoramic views of the surrounding countryside, including the Twelve Bens Mountain range and the Atlantic coastline.

Visitor Centre: The park's Visitor Centre serves as an ideal starting point. It includes information on the park's flora and animals, interactive displays, and a tearoom.

Walking paths: Connemara National Park provides multiple walking paths catering to all fitness levels. The Diamond Hill Trails, in particular, provide possibilities for shorter strolls or more demanding excursions.

Wildlife and Flora: Keep a watch out for Connemara horses, red deer, and a variety of bird species. The Park is home to rich plant life, including rare orchids and heathers.

Kylemore Abbey and Victorian Walled Garden: While not part of the national park, adjacent Kylemore Abbey is a must-visit destination. Explore the beautiful abbey, Victorian Walled Garden, and appreciate the gorgeous location alongside a lake.

Outdoor Activities: Connemara National Park offers options for outdoor lovers, including hillwalking, birding, and photography. The diversified landscape guarantees a satisfying experience for nature enthusiasts.

Information and Guided Tours: The Visitor Centre gives information on the park's characteristics, and guided tours are offered for anyone wanting a more in-depth understanding of the flora, animals, and history of the region.

Accessibility: Some pathways are wheelchair accessible, making the park inclusive for a broad spectrum of people.

Visitor Experience: Immerse yourself in the natural beauty, solitude, and fresh air of Connemara National Park. The Park allows reconnecting with nature and discovering the rugged appeal of Ireland's west coast.

Tips for the Visit:

Weather Considerations: Be prepared for changing weather conditions, including rain. Wear proper attire and sturdy footwear.

Visitor Centre: Start your journey in the Visitor Centre to acquire information, maps, and view exhibitions.

Photography: Don't forget your camera or smartphone — the sceneries give many picture possibilities.

Connemara National Park is a destination for anyone seeking outdoor experiences, tranquil treks, and an intimate touch with Ireland's wild beauty. Whether you're a wildlife fanatic or a casual tourist, the park provides an immersive experience in a unique and pure setting.

Galway City Highlights

Galway City, situated on Ireland's west coast, is a bustling and culturally diverse city with a distinct combination of history and modernity. Here are some highlights to discover in Galway City:

Eyre Square: Start your trip with Eyre Square, a key center surrounded by shops, cafés, and historic sites. The plaza is a popular gathering spot and a bustling location for activities.

Shop Street and Latin Quarter: Wander along the pedestrianized Shop Street, dotted with colorful stores, buskers, and vibrant ambiance. Explore the Latin Quarter, noted for its quaint alleyways, old bars, and unique stores.

Galway Cathedral: Visit the Galway Cathedral, an outstanding edifice with beautiful architecture. The church is recognized for its mosaics, artwork, and tranquil atmosphere.

Spanish Arch: Explore the famous Spanish Arch, part of the city's medieval fortifications. The arch overlooks the River Corrib and is a wonderful site for a leisurely walk.

Claddagh Village: Discover the adjacent Claddagh Village, famed for the distinctive Claddagh Ring. Enjoy views of Galway Bay and discover the maritime traditions of the region.

Salthill Promenade: Head to Salthill Promenade, a lovely seaside promenade along Galway Bay. Enjoy views of the

Atlantic Ocean, the Cliffs of Moher on a clear day, and the bustling atmosphere of Salthill.

Galway City Museum: Immerse yourself in Galway's history at the Galway City Museum. The museum offers exhibits on the city's archaeology, history, and culture.

Kirwan's Road: Stroll down Kirwan's Lane, a lovely medieval road in the center of the city. Discover traditional taverns, artisan stores, and the ancient Lynch's Castle.

Nimmo's Pier: For a calm getaway, visit Nimmo's Pier beside the River Corrib. It's a quiet area with views of the lake and the renowned Galway Cathedral.

Quay Street: Experience the bustling atmosphere of Quay Street, replete with taverns, restaurants, and live music. This region is noted for its bustling nightlife.

Galway Arts Festival: If coming in July, don't miss the Galway International Arts Festival. The city comes alive with performances, exhibits, and cultural events.

Galway Bay and the Long Stroll: Enjoy a stroll along the Long Walk, a scenic region along Galway Bay. Admire the colorful mansions and observe the boats in the port.

Traditional Music Sessions: Galway is known for its traditional music culture. Experience live sessions at the city's bars, where local musicians display their abilities.

Galway City's highlights embody the spirit of Ireland's west coast, merging historic beauty with a modern flair. Whether you're meandering through ancient streets, experiencing live music, or taking in seaside vistas, Galway provides a memorable and exciting experience.

Accommodation Options

Galway City provides a broad choice of housing alternatives to suit different interests and budgets. Here are suggestions across several categories:

Luxury Hotels:

The G Hotel:

a. **Location:** Wellpark, Dublin Road, Galway
b. **Description:** A premium hotel recognized for its contemporary design, spa facilities, and superb food. The G Hotel delivers a beautiful and pleasant stay.

The Galmont Hotel & Spa:

a. **Location:** Lough Atalia Road, Galway

b. **Description:** Situated on the shoreline, this premium hotel provides large rooms, a spa, and lovely views of Lough Atalia.

Boutique Hotels: The House Hotel:

a. **Location:** Spanish Parade, Galway

b. **Description:** A boutique hotel with trendy décor, situated in the heart of Galway's Latin Quarter. The House Hotel delivers a combination of contemporary comfort and historic charm.

The Twelve Hotel:

a. **Location:** Barna Village, Galway

b. **Description:** A boutique hotel a short drive from Galway, The Twelve Hotel is noted for its distinctive decor, superb dining choices, and individual service.

Mid-Range Hotels:

Jurys Inn Galway:

a. **Location:** Quay Street, Galway

b. Description: Centrally situated, Jurys Inn provides pleasant accommodations and is within walking distance of several sights, including the Spanish Arch and Shop Street.

Harbour Hotel:

a. Location: New Dock Road, Galway

b. Description: Overlooking Galway Harbor, Harbour Hotel offers contemporary lodgings with an emphasis on comfort and convenience.

Budget-Friendly Options:

Snoozles Hostel:

a. Location: Forster Street, Galway

b. Description: A budget-friendly hostel in a prime location, Snoozles provides dormitory and individual rooms. Ideal for tourists searching for economic and social accommodation.

Barnacles Hostel:

a. Location: Quay Street, Galway

b. Description: Another popular hostel situated on busy Quay Street, Barnacles offers a pleasant environment and budget-friendly dormitory alternatives.

Self-Catering Apartments:

The Western Hotel Apartments:

a. **Location:** Prospect Hill, Galway
b. **Description:** Conveniently situated in Eyre Square, The Western Hotel Apartments provide self-catering accommodation with contemporary conveniences.

Airbnb:

Description: Explore a range of apartments, residences, and unusual lodgings with Airbnb. This option enables you to explore local communities and tailor your stay.

Tips for Booking:

Book in Advance: Secure your accommodation in advance, particularly during high seasons or events.Read Reviews: Check reviews on sites like TripAdvisor or Booking.com to verify the lodging fits your expectations.

Location: Consider the closeness of the hotel to your planned activities and attractions.

Galway City's lodging choices appeal to a variety of interests, from luxury hotels to budget-friendly hostels. Whether you're seeking a central location, waterfront views, or a quaint boutique experience, Galway has numerous alternatives for a pleasant stay.

Chapter Four: Cork - A City of Culture, History, and Vibrancy

Blarney Castle

Blarney Castle, situated near Cork in County Cork, Ireland, is a medieval fortification that draws tourists from across the globe. Here's a guide to touring the lovely Blarney Castle:

Location: Blarney, County Cork, Ireland

Description: Situated roughly 8 kilometers northwest of Cork City, Blarney Castle is readily accessible and well-signposted.

The Famous Blarney Stone: The principal attraction of Blarney Castle is the famed Blarney Stone. According to folklore, kissing the stone endows the kisser with the "gift of the gab" or brilliant speech.

Castle and Gardens: Explore the historic Blarney Castle, dating back to the 15th century, and climb to the top for panoramic views of the surrounding area. The castle is surrounded by stunning gardens including distinctive rock formations and themed sections.

Blarney House: Adjacent to the castle lies Blarney House, a large home with stunning grounds. While the home may not always be available to the public, the gardens are worth investigating.

Poison Garden: Blarney Castle is home to a Poison Garden, showcasing a variety of deadly plants. Guided tours give insights into the harmful qualities of these plants.

Blarney Woollen Mills: Visit the neighboring Blarney Woollen Mills, a historic Irish establishment selling a broad choice of traditional Irish items, including woolens, crafts, and souvenirs.

Walking paths: Enjoy the picturesque walking paths surrounding the castle and grounds. The rich foliage and quiet environment make for a great excursion.

Events and Activities: Check for special events or activities taking place at Blarney Castle, like as historical reenactments, storytelling, or cultural festivities.

Visitor Center:mThe Visitor Center offers information, tickets, and amenities. It's a wonderful starting place for your tour of Blarney Castle.

Time of Visit: Consider the time of your visit. While Blarney Castle is attractive year-round, spring and summer bring vivid blossoms to the grounds.

Tips for the Visit:

Kissing the Blarney Stone: If you elect to kiss the Blarney Stone, be prepared for an unusual experience as you bend backward over a parapet to reach the stone.

Comfy Footwear: Wear comfy shoes ideal for walking and climbing stairs.

Photography: Don't forget your camera or smartphone to capture the stunning sights and historic surroundings.

Blarney Castle, with its famed stone and scenic environs, provides a fascinating combination of history, tradition, and natural beauty. Whether you're pulled by the attraction of the Blarney Stone or the attractiveness of the castle grounds, a visit to Blarney Castle gives a typical Irish experience.

English Market

The English Market, situated in the center of Cork City, is a dynamic and historic market that has been drawing people for generations. Here's a guide to experiencing the gastronomic pleasures of the English Market:

Location: Princes Street, Cork City, County Cork, Ireland

Description: Situated in the city center, the English Market is readily accessible and is a focal point of Cork's culinary scene.

History: The English Market has a rich history stretching back to 1788. It has been a magnet for local merchants, artists, and food producers for years.

Fresh Produce: Stroll through the market's busy aisles to uncover a variety of fresh produce, including fruits, vegetables, meats, cheeses, and seafood. The market is recognized for its high-quality, locally sourced items.

Artisanal items: Explore the booths providing artisanal items, including homemade chocolates, pastries, bread, and local crafts. It's a paradise for individuals seeking distinctive and original Irish items.

Seafood booths: Indulge in the fresh seafood options, with booths showing a range of fish, shellfish, and smoked delicacies. The English Market's seafood is especially known for its quality.

Butchers and Meat items: Visit the market's traditional butchers for a range of locally produced meats, sausages, and cured items. Knowledgeable merchants might give advice and culinary ideas.

Cheese Stalls: Delight in the assortment of Irish cheeses offered at the market. The cheese vendors provide a broad assortment, from creamy bries to matured cheddars.

Cafés and Food booths: Enjoy a meal or snack at one of the market's cafés or food booths. Whether it's a hearty Irish stew, a gourmet sandwich, or a pastry, there's something to satisfy every taste.

Culinary Events: Check for culinary events or demonstrations that may be taking place in the market. It's a chance to learn more about Irish food and meet with local cooks.

Shopping Experience: Immerse yourself in the colorful ambiance of the English Market. Engage with the friendly sellers, learn about their goods, and relish the sensory experience of this ancient marketplace.

Tips for the Visit:

Opening Hours: Check the market's opening hours, since they may fluctuate during the week.

Cash: While many businesses accept card payments, having some cash on hand might be useful.

Explore Nearby: The English Market is situated in a key section of Cork City, making it convenient to visit neighboring sights, shops, and cafés.

The English Market provides a gastronomic excursion, enabling tourists to sample the flavors of Cork and feel the warmth of its food culture. Whether you're a culinary connoisseur, a visitor seeking local experiences, or someone shopping for high-quality products, a visit to the English Market is a must while in Cork.

University College Cork

University College Cork (UCC) is one of Ireland's major institutions, noted for its academic brilliance, active campus culture, and rich history. Here's a guide to exploring UCC:

Location: Western Road, Cork City, County Cork, Ireland

Description: UCC is located in the city center, making it conveniently accessible. The college is noted for its lovely location along the River Lee.

History: Founded in 1845, UCC has a long and storied history. The university has played a vital role in education, research, and the cultural life of Cork and Ireland.

Quad and Main Campus: The main campus contains a magnificent Quad, surrounded by historic buildings, notably the famed Main Quadrangle. The Quad is a gorgeous area for students and tourists alike.

Crawford Observatory: The Crawford Observatory, situated on campus, provides a unique chance for stargazing and astronomical observation. Check for public activities or lectures at the observatory.

Glucksman Gallery: The Lewis Glucksman Gallery is an award-winning modern art gallery situated on the UCC campus. It presents a varied variety of temporary exhibits and cultural activities.

Honan Chapel: Visit the Honan Chapel, a finely designed Gothic Revival chapel on campus. It is noted for its architectural splendor and stained-glass windows.

University College Cork Library: The Boole Library is the primary library of UCC, holding an enormous collection of books, periodicals, and digital resources. It's a centre for intellectual research and learning.

Tyndall National Institute: The Tyndall National Institute, situated on the UCC campus, specializes in research in electronics, photonics, and nanotechnology. It works with business and academics.

Cork University Hospital (CUH): UCC is associated with Cork University Hospital, a significant teaching hospital. This relationship provides prospects for medical and healthcare research and teaching.

Cork School of Music: The Cork School of Music, part of UCC, is a center for music instruction and performance. Check for concerts, recitals, and events highlighting the skills of students and teachers.

Clubs and organizations: UCC offer a dynamic student life with various clubs and organizations embracing a broad variety of interests, from sports and arts to cultural and intellectual endeavors.

The Quad Food Court: The Quad Food Court is a popular area for students to get a lunch or snack. It provides a range of solutions to suit diverse preferences.

Tips for Visitors:

Guided Tours: Check whether guided tours of the UCC campus are offered to acquire insights into its history and significant features.

Public Events: Look out for public events, lectures, or cultural performances occurring on campus during your stay.

University College Cork's campus combines a combination of historical beauty and contemporary amenities, producing a favorable atmosphere for study, research, and cultural participation. Whether you're a prospective student, a guest, or someone interested in the cultural and intellectual life of Cork, UCC provides a distinctive and fascinating experience.

Accommodation Options

Cork City provides a choice of housing alternatives to meet diverse tastes and budgets. Here are suggestions across several categories:

Luxury Hotels:

The River Lee Hotel:

a. **Location:** Western Road, Cork City

b. **Description:** A magnificent hotel with contemporary conveniences, The River Lee Hotel provides spectacular views of the River Lee. It's centrally positioned, making it ideal for touring the city.

The Montenotte Hotel:

a. **Location:** Middle Glanmire Road, Cork City

b. **Description:** This upmarket hotel delivers a combination of modern flair and historic charm. Enjoy magnificent views of the city from its lofty elevation.

Boutique Hotels:

The Dean Cork:

a. **Location:** Horgans Quay, Cork City

b. **Description:** A fashionable boutique hotel with attractive decor and comfy accommodations. It's situated in the city center and provides a unique and dynamic environment.

The River Lee Townhouse:

a. **Location:** Western Road, Cork City

b. **Description:** A boutique-style lodging next to The River Lee Hotel, the townhouse offers a more personal environment while still giving access to the hotel's facilities.

Mid-Range Hotels:

Maldron Hotel South Mall:

a. **Location:** South Mall, Cork City

b. **Description:** A well-appointed hotel in the heart of Cork, Maldron Hotel South Mall provides comfortable accommodations and is within walking distance of famous attractions.

Jurys Inn Cork:

a. **Location:** Anderson's Quay, Cork City

b. **Description:** Centrally situated, Jurys Inn Cork has contemporary rooms and is near sites such as the English Market and St. Fin Barre's Cathedral.

Budget-Friendly Options:

Sheilas Tourist Hostel:

a. **Location:** Belgrave Place, Wellington Road, Cork City

b. **Description:** A budget-friendly hostel with a warm environment. Sheilas Tourist Hostel is well-positioned for exploring Cork on foot.

Kinlay House Cork:

a. **Location:** Bob and Joan's Walk, Shandon, Cork City

b. **Description:** Situated in the historic Shandon neighborhood, Kinlay House Cork is a budget-friendly hostel providing both dormitory and private rooms.

Self-Catering Apartments:

The Kingsley Hotel Apartments:

    a. **Location:** Victoria Cross, Cork City

    b. **Description:** If you prefer self-catering choices, The Kingsley Hotel Apartments offer large and well-equipped flats near the University College Cork campus.

Airbnb:

Description: Explore numerous apartments, residences, and unique lodgings with Airbnb. This choice gives flexibility and the possibility to visit local communities.

Tips for Booking:

Book in Advance: Especially during high seasons or events, arranging accommodation in advance is important.

Check Reviews: Before booking, check reviews on sites like TripAdvisor or Booking.com to verify the hotel fits your expectations.

Location Matters: Consider the location related to your intended activities to improve your stay.

Cork City's numerous lodging choices appeal to different interests, whether you're seeking luxury, boutique charm, mid-range comfort, or budget-friendly alternatives. Choose lodging depending on your goals, whether it's closeness to attractions, style, or economic concerns.

Chapter Five: Belfast - A City of History, Culture, and Resilience

Titanic Belfast

Titanic Belfast is a world-renowned tourist experience that brings to life the tale of the RMS Titanic, the legendary ship that tragically perished on her maiden voyage in 1912. Here's a guide to touring Titanic Belfast:

Location: Queen's Road, Titanic Quarter, Belfast, Northern Ireland

Description: Titanic Belfast is located in the historic Titanic Quarter, overlooking the slipways where the Titanic and her sister ship, Olympic, were built.

Exterior Architecture: Marvel at the stunning architecture of Titanic Belfast. The building's architecture mimics the ship's hull and has stunning glass facades, reflecting the surrounding landscape.

Nine Galleries: Explore the nine interpretative and interactive galleries within Titanic Belfast. Each gallery is devoted to a distinct element of the Titanic narrative, from its building to its ill-fated maiden voyage.

Shipyard Ride: Begin your tour with the Shipyard Ride, an entertaining experience that takes you around the shipyard, enabling you to observe the building process of the Titanic.

The Launch Gallery: Discover the excitement and anticipation surrounding the Titanic's launch in The Launch Gallery. Multimedia displays and exhibitions highlight the majesty of the ship's debut.

The Maiden Voyage: Learn about the preparations, luxury, and obstacles experienced during the Titanic's first journey in The First Journey Gallery. The collection gives insights into living on board the ship.

The Sinking: Experience the horrific night of April 14-15, 1912, in The Sinking Gallery. The exhibit carefully illustrates the events leading to the terrible sinking of the Titanic.

The Aftermath: Explore the Aftermath Gallery, which digs into the aftermath of the accident, including rescue attempts, investigations, and the influence on marine safety standards.

Titanic Beneath: Descend to the ground level to view Titanic Beneath, an interactive exhibit that chronicles the findings of the Titanic disaster on the ocean below.

SS Nomadic: Adjacent to Titanic Belfast sits SS Nomadic, the sole surviving White Star Line ship. Take a guided tour of this tender ship that carried people to the Titanic.

Visitor Facilities: Titanic Belfast provides tourist amenities, including a gift store, eateries, and outdoor areas. The building's higher stories give magnificent views of the Titanic Quarter and Belfast Lough.

Tips for the Visit:

Book Tickets in Advance: To secure entrance and avoid lengthy waits, consider ordering tickets online in advance.

Audio Guides: Opt for audio guides to improve your comprehension of the exhibits and the Titanic tale.

Allow Sufficient Time: Plan to spend a few hours visiting Titanic Belfast fully.

Titanic Belfast remains as a somber homage to the Titanic's heritage and the lives lost on that dreadful night. The museum's immersive displays, inventive architecture, and historical relevance make it a must-visit location for people interested in maritime history and the narrative of the "unsinkable" ship.

Belfast City Hall

Belfast City Hall is a stately and famous structure situated in the center of Belfast, Northern Ireland. Here's a guide to explore this historic and architectural gem:

Location: Donegall Square, Belfast, Northern Ireland

Description: Belfast City Hall is strategically positioned in the center of the city, in Donegall Square.

Architecture: Marvel at the great architecture of Belfast City Hall, built by architect Sir Alfred Brumwell Thomas. The building's notable characteristics include a Baroque Revival design with a central dome and classical statues.

Titanic Memorial Garden: Explore the Titanic Memorial Garden situated on the grounds of City Hall. The garden remembers the people lost in the sinking of the RMS Titanic and comprises sculptures and inscriptions.

Great Hall: Visit the Great Hall within Belfast City Hall, a beautiful hall filled with marble, stained glass, and a great staircase. The Great Hall holds numerous events, including concerts and civic ceremonies.

City Council Chamber: Take a guided tour to discover the City Council Chamber, where important decisions are made. Admire the exquisite woodwork and learn about the history of Belfast's government.

Titanic Memorial: Pay your respects at the Titanic Memorial, a significant landmark in the City Hall's grounds. The monument recalls the engineers who lost their lives during the building of the Titanic.

Public Events: Check for public events and ceremonies that may be taking place at City Hall. The edifice typically acts as a background for cultural festivities, concerts, and meetings.

Grounds and Gardens: Enjoy the well-maintained grounds and gardens around Belfast City Hall. The region offers a **calm respite in the center of the hectic metropolis.**

Linen Hall Library: Nearby, you'll discover the Linen Hall Library, one of Belfast's oldest libraries. Explore its holdings, which include historic books, manuscripts, and antiquities.

Festivals and Markets: City Hall generally acts as a focal point for festivals, markets, and events. Check the local calendar for any occurrences during your stay.

Tips for the Visit:

Guided Tours: Consider taking a guided tour of Belfast City Hall for a more in-depth knowledge of its history and importance.

Photography: Capture the amazing architecture and features both inside and outside the structure.

Events Calendar: Check the events calendar to see if any special events or exhibits are planned during your stay.

Belfast City Hall stands as a symbol of civic pride and a tribute to the city's rich heritage. Whether you're interested in architecture, and history, or just enjoying the gorgeous surroundings, a visit to Belfast City Hall is a wonderful experience.

Political Murals

Belfast is famed for its political murals that cover the city's walls, presenting a visual narrative of its complicated history and geopolitical battles. Here's a guide to visiting the political murals in Belfast:

Murals Locations: Political murals are distributed throughout numerous districts in Belfast, with noteworthy concentrations in locations like Falls Road and Shankill Road. These murals generally represent the opinions of the communities in which they are placed.

Falls Road Murals: Falls Road is home to a substantial number of political murals that reflect many parts of Northern Ireland's history, including the Troubles and the battle for civil rights.

Shankill Road Murals: Shankill Road has murals that portray the Unionist and Loyalist community's beliefs. These paintings frequently highlight historical events and personalities related to their identity.

International Wall: The International Wall, situated on Divis Street, serves as a canvas for political murals that address worldwide concerns, solidarity movements, and demonstrations of support for diverse causes.

Peace Walls: While not murals in the usual sense, the Peace Walls in Belfast are huge obstacles that divide various groups. These walls are commonly adorned with words of hope, peace, and remembering.

Bogside Murals in Derry: While not in Belfast, the city of Derry (Londonderry) is notable for its collection of political murals in the Bogside region. These paintings reflect events such as Bloody Sunday and the civil rights struggle.

West Belfast Mural Tours: Consider taking a guided mural tour, such as the West Belfast Mural Tours, to acquire insights into the historical background and tales behind the murals. Local guides give vital views on the Troubles and the peace process.

Issues and Symbolism: Political murals in Belfast generally address issues such as identity, nationalism, the Troubles, and the peace process. They serve as a sort of public art that represents the community's collective memories and ambitions.

Evolving Artistic Landscape: The political murals in Belfast are not static; they develop throughout time. New murals may replace older ones, and the topics may evolve to represent shifting viewpoints and cultural advances.

Respect Local Sensitivities: When examining political murals, be cognizant of the local sensitivities and the historical context. Approach the work with an open mind and a readiness to learn about the varied tales.

Tips for the Visit:

Guided Tours: Consider attending a guided mural tour to acquire more insights into the history and importance of the paintings.

Respectful Photography: If shooting images, be respectful of the murals and the communities they represent. Avoid photographing private dwellings and be aware of local neighbors.

Belfast's political murals give a unique viewpoint on the city's history, creating a visual discourse on complicated themes. While studying these murals, visitors may obtain a greater knowledge of the issues encountered by the communities and the continuous road toward reconciliation and peace.

Accommodation Options

Belfast provides a range of housing alternatives to suit various interests and budgets. Here are suggestions across many categories:

Luxury Hotels:

The Merchant Hotel:

a. **Location:** Skipper Street, Belfast

b. **Description:** A 5-star luxury hotel in a former bank building, The Merchant Hotel features exquisite rooms, a rooftop gym, and a famous spa. It's centrally positioned, making it ideal for touring the city.

Europa Hotel:

a. **Location:** Great Victoria Street, Belfast

b. **Description:** Known as the "most bombed hotel in Europe" during the Troubles, Europa Hotel is now a luxury and historic lodging choice with contemporary conveniences and a prominent city center position.

Boutique Hotels:

Ten Square Hotel:

a. **Location:** Donegall Square South, Belfast

b. **Description:** A trendy boutique hotel situated in the center of Belfast, Ten Square Hotel provides sleek rooms and a rooftop terrace with panoramic views of the city.

The Fitzwilliam Hotel Belfast:

a. **Location:** Great Victoria Street, Belfast

b. **Description:** A modern boutique hotel near the Grand Opera House, The Fitzwilliam Hotel has elegant décor, sophisticated restaurants, and large accommodations.

Mid-Range Hotels:

Malmaison Belfast:

a. **Location:** Victoria Street, Belfast

b. **Description:** Situated in a converted seed warehouse, Malmaison Belfast is a beautiful mid-range hotel with modern décor, pleasant rooms, and a cafe offering gourmet food.

Clayton Hotel Belfast:

a. **Location:** Ormeau Avenue, Belfast

b. **Description:** A contemporary hotel with a central position, Clayton Hotel Belfast provides pleasant rooms, a fitness facility, and a restaurant with an emphasis on local food.

Budget-Friendly Options:

Bullitt Hotel:

a. **Location:** Ann Street, Belfast

b. **Description:** Bullitt Hotel is a modern and budget-friendly alternative with tiny rooms, a rooftop garden, and a bustling bar. It's strategically positioned, near to numerous attractions.

ETAP Hotel Belfast:

a. **Location:** Talbot Street, Belfast

b. **Description:** As a budget-friendly alternative, ETAP Hotel Belfast provides modest and contemporary rooms with the necessary conveniences. It's a realistic alternative for tourists on a budget.

Self-Catering Apartments:

Dream Apartments:

a. **Location:** Obel Tower, Belfast

b. **Description:** Dream Apartments provides serviced apartments with cooking amenities in the Obel Tower. The apartments give a home-like feel and spectacular city views.

Titanic Apartments:

a. **Location:** The Arc, Belfast

b. **Description:** Located in the Titanic Quarter, Titanic Apartments provides self-catering accommodation with contemporary conveniences. It's near to Titanic Belfast and other attractions.

Hostels:

Vagabonds Belfast:

a. **Location:** Fitzwilliam Street, Belfast

b. Description: Vagabonds Belfast is a welcoming hostel providing dormitory and private rooms. It offers a shared kitchen, and social rooms, and is within walking distance of city center attractions.

Lagan Backpackers:

    a. Location: Laganbank Road, Belfast

    b. Description: Lagan Backpackers is a budget-friendly hostel with a casual environment, offering dormitory accommodation. It's located beside the River Lagan.

Tips for Booking:

Book in Advance: Secure your accommodation in advance, particularly during high seasons or events.

Read Reviews: Check reviews on sites like TripAdvisor or Booking.com to verify the lodging fits your expectations.

Location: Consider the closeness of the hotel to your planned activities and attractions.

Belfast's housing choices appeal to a variety of interests, from luxury hotels to budget-friendly hostels. Whether you're looking for a central location, historical charm, or contemporary conveniences, Belfast has numerous alternatives for a pleasant stay.

Chapter Six: Exploring the Countryside

Ring of Kerry

Nestled in the stunning surroundings of Ireland's southwest, the Ring of Kerry serves as a tribute to the country's natural beauty and rich cultural past. This classic beautiful route, surrounding the Iveragh Peninsula, takes guests on a trip through gorgeous towns, historic sites, and awe-inspiring panoramas. With each twist and turn, the Ring of Kerry unveils a tale that ties together the past, present, and the everlasting charm of Ireland's landscape.

Route & Highlights: The Ring of Kerry spans around 179 kilometers (111 miles) along meandering roads, showcasing a rich tapestry of scenery. The trek normally starts and finishes in the town of Killarney, making it accessible for people touring from the famed Killarney National Park. As you begin on this round journey, various attractions await, enticing investigation.

Killarney to Kenmare:

Starting from Killarney, the path meanders via the famed Muckross House and grounds, a Victorian home surrounded by immaculate grounds and the dazzling waters of Muckross Lake. From there, the route leads to Ladies View, a panoramic viewpoint that captivates with its sweeping views of the Lakes of Killarney and the MacGillycuddy's Reeks Mountain range.

Continuing into Kenmare, a picturesque town perched at the tip of Kenmare Bay, tourists may explore its colorful streets, browse local stores, and appreciate the gastronomic pleasures provided by its cafes.

Kenmare to Sneem:

Leaving Kenmare, the route widens to show the mythical Gleninchaquin Park, where walking paths bring explorers through magnificent trees, past waterfalls, and beside quiet lakes. Sneem, renowned as the "Knot in the Ring," awaits with its distinctive architecture and colorful atmosphere. The hamlet is home to the Sneem Sculpture Park, presenting a variety of intriguing sculptures among gorgeous settings.

Sneem to Waterville:

As the road makes its way into Waterville, passengers are treated to the magnificent coastline vistas of Derrynane Bay. The magnificent Derrynane House, previously the home of Daniel O'Connell, the "Liberator," looks into Ireland's political past.

Waterville, set on the banks of Ballinskelligs Bay, has a fascinating history connected with the Atlantic Ocean. The town has long been a favored refuge for artists and celebrities, attracted to its beautiful beauty and calm environment.

Waterville to Cahersiveen:

The trip continues down the coast to Cahersiveen, a town rich in history and a gateway to the Skellig Islands. The Cahersiveen Heritage Center gives insights into the region's past, especially its relation to the Great Famine and the transatlantic migration that followed.

Cahersiveen to Glenbeigh:

As the Ring proceeds, the scenery alters, displaying the raw beauty of the Ballaghisheen Pass. Majestic mountains and peaceful lakes define this portion of the tour. Glenbeigh, located at the northern extremity of the Iveragh Peninsula, gives access to the picturesque Rossbeigh Beach and the historic Glenbeigh Towers.

Glenbeigh to Killorglin:

The route carries passengers via the scenic town of Caherdaniel, with its old Derrynane Abbey, before arriving at Killorglin. Known for its vibrant atmosphere, Killorglin holds the annual Puck Fair, one of Ireland's oldest festivals, honoring local culture and customs.

Practical Tips:

Timing and Weather: The greatest time to visit the Ring of Kerry is during the gentler seasons of spring and fall when the landscapes explode with color.

Weather conditions in Ireland may be unpredictable, so it's advised to carry layers and waterproof gear.

Transportation: While driving affords freedom, consider taking guided tours for insights into local history and culture.

Bus trips and bicycle alternatives are available for those who prefer not to drive.

Accommodations: Accommodations along the route vary from beautiful bed & breakfasts to luxurious hotels, giving a variety of alternatives for various budgets.

Booking lodgings in advance, particularly during high seasons, is suggested.

Local Cuisine: Sample local foods in the communities along the road, experiencing the flavors of Irish cuisine.

Many places take pleasure in utilizing fresh, locally sourced food.

The Ring of Kerry is not simply a drive; it's an expedition into the heart of Ireland's southwest, showing the soul-stirring beauty and cultural depth of the province. As the road unfolds, each sight and settlement tell a narrative, creating a tapestry of experiences that stays in the hearts of those who embark on this spectacular trip. Whether attracted by the seaside views, historical sites, or the warm hospitality of the local villages, the Ring of Kerry is an invitation to immerse oneself in the timeless attraction of Ireland's countryside.

The Burren

Nestled along the western coast of Ireland, the Burren stands as a geological wonder and archaeological treasure trove, enticing tourists with its unique combination of karst landscapes, ancient ruins, and uncommon vegetation. Covering around 250 square kilometers in County Clare, the Burren is a location where time appears to stand still, beckoning visitors to solve its secrets and immerse themselves in a scenery unlike any other.

Geological Wonders:

At first look, the Burren may seem bleak, with its wide stretches of limestone pavement generating an unearthly and even lunar-like atmosphere. The name "Burren" itself is derived from the Irish word "Boíreann," meaning a rocky location. The karst topography is characterized by crisscrossing fissures, known as grikes, and the rocky slabs, or clints, that develop between them.

a. Limestone Pavement:

As you travel the Burren, the limestone pavement under your feet gives testament to the forces of erosion that have formed the terrain over thousands of years. The distinctive pattern of grikes and clints produces a mosaic of natural cracks, displaying the delicate dance between water, wind, and time.

b. A Tapestry of Wildflowers:

Despite its obviously hostile aspect, the Burren holds an incredible assortment of plant life, earning it the status as a Special Area of Conservation. From April to September, the limestone fractures explode into color with a tapestry of wildflowers, including uncommon species such as the spring gentian, bloody cranesbill, and orchids. The Burren's flora is a tribute to the persistence and adaptation of nature in the face of harsh circumstances.

c. Poulnabrone Dolmen:

Among the limestone expanses, the old Poulnabrone Dolmen stands as a sentry from Ireland's Neolithic past. Dating back to roughly 3600 BCE, this megalithic tomb consists of a massive capstone supported by two gateway stones, creating a hauntingly beautiful and intriguing sight.

Poulnabrone Dolmen is a monument to the lasting skill of Ireland's early people.

Archaeological Riches:

Beyond its physical beauties, the Burren has a plethora of archaeological relics that give an insight into Ireland's prehistoric and medieval past.

a. Ancient Forts:

The Burren is littered with relics of old forts, such as Caherconnell and Leamaneh Castle. These stone constructions, located on lofty heights, give insights into the defensive systems of early settlers and medieval rulers.

b. Kilfenora Cathedral:

Kilfenora, a picturesque town in the middle of the Burren, is home to the old Kilfenora Cathedral. Dating back to the 12th century, the cathedral's beautiful stone carvings and medieval architecture remind of a period when the Burren was a center of religious activity.

c. Ailwee Cave:

Delve under the surface to discover Ailwee Cave, a subterranean treasure hidden amid the Burren. This cave system provides a guided trek through lighted chambers, exhibiting amazing formations moulded by the passage of time.

Burren in Bloom Festival:

The Burren's floral extravaganza is honoured yearly via the Burren in Bloom Festival. This festival, held in May, shows the brilliant wildflowers that cover the area, drawing botanists, nature lovers, and inquisitive tourists eager to experience the Burren in its full blooming grandeur.

Exploring the Burren:

a. Walking Trails:

Lace up your hiking boots and explore the Burren on foot. Several walking routes, including as the Burren Way and the Mullaghmore Loop, bring you through varied landscapes, affording encounters with ancient ruins, panoramic panoramas, and the delicate beauty of the Burren's flora.

b. Interpretative Centers:

Visit the Burren and Cliffs of Moher Geopark Visitor Center and the Burren Center in Kilfenora for insights into the region's geology, vegetation, and cultural history. Interactive exhibitions and guided tours give a fuller knowledge of the Burren's complex nature.

c. Guided Tours:

Join a guided tour led by skilled local guides who can explain tales of the Burren's history, point out uncommon plant species, and expose the hidden jewels strewn throughout this ancient environment.

Conservation and Sustainability:

Recognizing the significance of conserving the Burren's unique ecology, conservation initiatives, and sustainable tourist practices are actively pushed. Visitors are advised to step softly, remain on authorised trails, and preserve the fragile balance of this amazing environment.

The Burren, with its karst landscapes, historic structures, and floral splendour, encourages guests to embark on a journey through time and nature. This magical location, where stone and blossom dwell in peace, serves as a tribute to the persistence of life and the continuing fascination of Ireland's natural beauty. Whether you explore its geological marvels, dig into its archaeological secrets, or just absorb the quietude of its wildflower-covered stretches, the Burren guarantees an amazing and immersive experience in the heart of the Emerald Isle.

Wicklow Mountains

Nestled just south of Dublin, the Wicklow Mountains unfurl as a natural marvel, giving a haven for nature enthusiasts, hikers, and those seeking tranquility in the untamed countryside. This expansive mountain range, often referred to as the "Garden of Ireland," captivates with its rugged peaks, tranquil lakes, and meandering trails that beckon adventurers into a realm of breathtaking landscapes and ancient history.

A Tapestry of Peaks and Valleys: The Wicklow Mountains, part of the broader Wicklow Uplands, have a diversified landscape that spans from gentle hills to towering peaks. Lugnaquilla, towering at 925 meters (3,035 ft), has the distinction of being the highest mountain in the range.

These mountains produce a stunning tapestry of heather-covered slopes, granite cliffs, and glacial valleys, producing a scene that is both magnificent and appealing.

Glendalough: A Valley of Two Lakes: At the heart of the Wicklow Mountains is Glendalough, a glacial valley famed for its two tranquil lakes, Upper and Lower Glendalough. This "Valley of Two Lakes" is home to one of Ireland's most significant monastic sites, where the ancient round tower stands as a sentinel of centuries past. The Glendalough Monastic Settlement, established by St. Kevin in the 6th century, comprises a collection of medieval structures, including churches and a cathedral, hidden among the serene environment.

Wicklow Way: A Hiker's Haven: For those keen to explore the Wicklow Mountains on foot, the Wicklow Way beckons as a hiker's sanctuary. Stretching over 130 kilometers (80 miles), this long-distance track snakes its way through the heart of the Alps, carrying hikers through different terrain and giving magnificent views of the surrounding area. The path is well-marked, enabling hikers to pick parts that meet their ability levels and time limits.

Powerscourt Estate: A Garden Oasis: Nestled amid the foothills of the Wicklow Mountains, Powerscourt Estate stands as a tribute to the beautiful marriage of natural beauty and human creativity. The estate comprises a beautiful home, elaborate grounds, and the majestic Powerscourt Waterfall, Ireland's tallest waterfall. The formal gardens, with their terraced lawns and blooming flowerbeds, provide a tranquil escape, while the nearby waterfall invites contemplation amid nature's grandeur.

Lough Tay: The Guinness Lake: Lough Tay, frequently known to as the "Guinness Lake" owing to its dark peaty waters and the white sandy beach resembling a pint of Guinness, is a gorgeous jewel set amid the highlands. The surrounding hills and trees form a lovely background, making Lough Tay a favorite location for photographers and those seeking a tranquil respite.

The Sally Gap: A Scenic Drive: The Sally Gap, a mountain pass snaking through the Wicklow Mountains, provides a picturesque journey that uncovers stunning views of the surrounding peaks and valleys. As you travel the twisting road, take in the huge expanses of heather-covered moors and the distant glacial lakes, providing a feeling of peace in the rough environment.

Ancient History: The Wicklow Mountains give evidence of Ireland's ancient past, with countless archaeological sites strewn throughout the countryside. The ancient passage tomb at Seefin and the monastery remains at Glendalough give insights into the life of early settlers and monks who sought comfort in these distant mountain retreats.

Wildlife and Biodiversity: The Wicklow Mountains house a vast variety of flora and wildlife, generating ecosystems ranging from heathlands to blanket bogs. The mountains are home to a variety of bird species, including peregrine falcons and merlins. Red deer and mountain hares roam the upland areas, adding to the untamed allure of the region.

Mount Usher Gardens: A Botanical Haven: Located near the town of Ashford, Mount Usher Gardens provides a botanical refuge where tourists may meander through stunning gardens, arboretums, and wooded regions. The meticulously manicured landscapes feature a diverse assortment of plant species, giving a calm escape among the lush splendor of the Wicklow Mountains.

Practical Tips for Exploration:

Hiking Preparations: If beginning on hiking routes, ensure you have the correct boots, weather-appropriate gear, and a map of the paths.

Guided Tours: Consider taking guided tours or hiring local guides to expand your awareness of the environmental and cultural characteristics of the Wicklow Mountains.

Weather Awareness: The weather in the mountains may be unpredictable, so be prepared for changes and check predictions before starting.

The Wicklow Mountains, with their sweeping panoramas and rich history, beckon adventurers to travel into a world of natural marvels. Whether trekking the Wicklow Way, discovering historic monastic ruins in Glendalough, or just appreciating the calm of Lough Tay, the mountains provide a tapestry of experiences that connect with the wild beauty of Ireland's "Garden." In the embrace of these peaks and valleys, travelers discover not only a refuge for outdoor activities but a sanctuary for the spirit among the majesty of nature.

Wild Atlantic Way

Stretching over 2,500 kilometers along the rocky western coastline of Ireland, the Wild Atlantic Way ranks as one of the world's most intriguing coastal drives. This epic journey uncovers a tapestry of stunning landscapes, quaint communities, and cultural treasures, encouraging guests to go on a road trip that evokes the wild spirit of the Atlantic Ocean. From the windswept cliffs of Donegal to the spectacular bays of Cork, the Wild Atlantic Way is a journey of discovery, displaying the raw beauty and rich legacy of Ireland's western frontier.

Starting Point: The Wild Atlantic Way officially starts in the northernmost county of Donegal at Malin Head, Ireland's most northerly point. Here, the craggy cliffs and huge seascapes set the tone for the dramatic adventure ahead. From Malin Head, the road meanders southward, presenting a coastline carved by the merciless powers of the Atlantic.

Slieve League Cliffs: One of the early attractions along the journey is Slieve League, home to some of the tallest coastal cliffs in Europe. Towering above the Atlantic, these spectacular cliffs give panoramic views of the ocean and the rough coastline below, delivering an awe-inspiring introduction to the raw splendor of the Wild Atlantic Way.

Donegal's Gaeltacht Region: As you visit the coastal communities of Donegal, you'll find the Gaeltacht, where the Irish language is spoken natively. Embrace the rich Gaelic culture, discover traditional music sessions, and sample local foods in the snug pubs that dot this lonely and gorgeous part of the road.

Connemara: The untamed Atlantic Way then travels south into Connemara, a province noted for its rough and untamed vistas. Connemara's diversified topography includes steep mountains, extensive bogs, and calm lakes. The route takes you via the famed Sky Road, where the vistas of the coastline and the Twelve Bens Mountain range are nothing short of stunning.

The Burren: Moving southward, the Wild Atlantic Way crosses the peculiar karst landscapes of the Burren in County Clare. Amidst limestone pavements, historic ruins, and rare wildflowers, the Burren provides a harsh but magnificent contrast to the coastal backdrop, beckoning exploration and contemplation.

Cliffs of Moher: A feature not to be missed, the Cliffs of Moher rise steeply from the Atlantic, reaching heights of almost 200 meters. The sweeping vistas along the cliff edge display the force and grandeur of the ocean, making it one of the most memorable destinations along the Wild Atlantic Way.

Galway and the Aran Islands: The bustling city of Galway, rich in culture and innovation, welcomes guests with its lively atmosphere and attractive streets. Nearby, the Aran Islands give a chance to go back in time, where traditional Irish life flourishes against a background of old forts and stunning scenery.

The Dingle Peninsula: As the voyage proceeds south, the Dingle Peninsula reveals its craggy shoreline and charming settlements. The Slea Head Drive offers breathtaking views of the Atlantic, the Blasket Islands, and ancient archaeological sites, providing a rich tapestry of history and natural beauty.

Ring of Kerry: The Wild Atlantic Way effortlessly blends with the legendary Ring of Kerry, where green slopes meet the thundering ocean. This segment of the trip uncovers lovely communities, ancient sites, and stunning scenery, including the Gap of Dunloe and the Lakes of Killarney.

Mizen Head and Cork: The southernmost parts of the Wild Atlantic Way led tourists to Mizen Head, giving panoramic views of the Atlantic Ocean and the renowned Mizen Bridge. Cork, Ireland's second-largest city, beckons with its nautical heritage, active cultural scene, and culinary environment that emphasizes local products and seafood.

Practical Tips for the Journey:

Timing and Weather: The Wild Atlantic Way is a year-round attraction, although weather conditions may be changeable. Spring and summer give longer days and warmer temperatures, while fall offers beautiful scenery.

Accommodations: Plan lodgings, particularly during high travel seasons. Options vary from quaint bed & breakfasts to luxurious hotels, giving numerous alternatives for different tastes and budgets.

Road Conditions: While the bulk of the trip is readily passable, certain small and curving roads may need cautious driving. Be mindful of local road conditions, particularly in more isolated regions.

Cultural Experiences: Embrace the local culture by attending traditional music sessions, eating local food, and mingling with the welcoming villages along the route.

Outdoor Activities: The Wild Atlantic Way provides a range of outdoor activities, from hiking and cycling to water-based excursions. Pack appropriately, including adequate footwear for exploring the varied terrain.

The Wild Atlantic Way is not merely a road trip; it's an immersive journey into the soul-stirring beauty of Ireland's western coastline. Whether negotiating the winding roads of Donegal, gazing on the Cliffs of Moher, or experiencing the lively culture of Galway, each length of the journey unveils a new chapter in the narrative of the Atlantic's wild embrace. As you explore this epic coastal trek, you'll see a scenery that has molded Irish history, inspired timeless tales, and continued to capture the hearts of those who embark on this remarkable voyage along the edge of the Atlantic.

Chapter Seven: Outdoor Activities

Hiking and Walking Trails

Ireland's rich landscapes and diversified topography offer an assortment of hiking and walking paths for outdoor lovers. Lace-up your boots and immerse yourself in the breathtaking surroundings of the Emerald Isle. Here are some prominent paths to explore:

The Wicklow Way (County Wicklow): Ireland's oldest waymarked route, the Wicklow Way, leads you through the "Garden of Ireland." The walk includes around 130 kilometers, crossing mountains, woods, and picturesque towns. Highlights include Glendalough, Glenmalure Valley, and Djouce Mountain.

Cliffs of Moher Coastal Walk (County Clare): This seaside route along the Cliffs of Moher gives amazing views of the Atlantic Ocean. The trek runs around 18 kilometers, beginning from Liscannor and going to Doolin. Marvel at the towering cliffs, seabird colonies, and the Aran Islands in the distance.

The Burren Way (County Clare): The Burren Way brings you through the spectacular limestone landscapes of the Burren area. This path, roughly 123 kilometers long, shows rich vegetation, old stone forts, and the intriguing Poulnabrone Dolmen.

The Causeway Coast Way (County Antrim): Experience Northern Ireland's gorgeous shoreline on the Causeway Coast Way. The path spans for around 53 kilometers, incorporating notable sights like the Giant's Causeway, Carrick-a-Rede Rope Bridge, and Dunluce Castle.

Connemara National Park (County Galway): Connemara's National Park provides a variety of walking pathways among mountains, bogs, and forests. Explore the Diamond Hill Loop for panoramic views of the Twelve Bens Mountain range and the Atlantic Ocean.

Slieve League Cliffs (County Donegal): Towering above the Atlantic, the Slieve League Cliffs offer a spectacular environment for hikers. The One Man's Pass route provides excellent coastline views, while the Pilgrim's Path brings you to the peak of Slieve League.

Glen of Aherlow Loop (County Tipperary): The Glen of Aherlow Loop provides a tranquil trek through forests, meadows, and along the Aherlow River. The track is around 35 kilometers in total, with multiple loop alternatives appealing to different fitness levels.

Gap of Dunloe (County Kerry): Nestled in the MacGillycuddy's Reeks Mountain range, the Gap of Dunloe is a tiny mountain pass. Hike or enjoy a traditional pony and trap ride through this gorgeous glacier valley, past lakes, bridges, and the Wishing Bridge.

The Kerry Way (County Kerry): One of Ireland's longest-defined routes, the Kerry Way provides a beautiful tour along the Iveragh Peninsula. Explore seaside pathways, picturesque towns, and alpine scenery, including the MacGillycuddy's Reeks.

Cuilcagh Boardwalk Trail (County Fermanagh): Popularly known as the "Stairway to Heaven," this boardwalk route brings you to the peak of Cuilcagh Mountain. The high path reduces environmental effects, and the views from the summit are breathtaking.

Mourne Wall Walk (County Down): Follow the Mourne Wall, a granite wall that spans the Mourne Mountains. This tough climb takes you to mountains like Slieve Donard, the highest peak in Northern Ireland.

The Dingle Way (County Kerry): The Dingle Way provides a spectacular coastal and alpine walk along the Dingle Peninsula. Highlights include Inch Beach, the Conor Pass, and the lovely town of Dingle.

Whether you're seeking seaside views, mountain vistas, or forest calm, Ireland's hiking and walking routes provide unique outdoor excursions. Lace on your hiking boots, take in the fresh air, and start on a tour through some of the world's most magnificent settings.

Golf Courses

Ireland features some of the world's most gorgeous and demanding golf courses, making it a golfer's heaven. With a blend of magnificent settings and world-class designs, these courses provide an exceptional golfing experience. Here are some prominent golf courses in Ireland:

Old Course at Ballybunion (County Kerry): A classic links course, Ballybunion's Old Course is noted for its tough layout and spectacular vistas of the Atlantic Ocean. Golfers traverse across towering dunes, undulating fairways, and tricky greens.

Royal County Down Golf Club (County Down): Set against the backdrop of the Mourne Mountains and Dundrum Bay, Royal County Down is routinely named among the greatest golf courses internationally. Its tough design and stunning setting attract golf fans from throughout the globe.

Lahinch Golf Club (County Clare): Lahinch, situated along the Wild Atlantic Way, is famed for its natural beauty and wild coastal winds. The Old Course offers undulating fairways and tough bunkers, delivering a thrilling game of golf.

Portmarnock Golf Club (County Dublin): Situated on a short tongue of shallow duneland, Portmarnock is a traditional links course. With tough bunkers and smart design, it poses a stiff challenge for players. The club has a lengthy history, going back to 1894.

Tralee Golf Club (County Kerry): Designed by Arnold Palmer, Tralee Golf Club is a visual beauty with panoramic vistas of the Atlantic. The course twists across dunes and provides a variety of hard holes, making it a great golfing experience.

Royal Portrush Golf Club (County Antrim): Home to The Open in 2019, Royal Portrush is a stunning links course along the Causeway Coast. The Dunluce Links boasts stunning dunes, tough holes, and beautiful vistas of the North Atlantic.

Doonbeg Golf Club (County Clare): Now known as Trump International Golf Links, Doonbeg has a links-style course that snakes over dunes and affords beautiful vistas of the Atlantic coastline. The course received remodeling and upgrades in recent years.

The K Club (County Kildare): Host of the 2006 Ryder Cup, The K Club is a premium golf resort with two championship courses - the Palmer Ryder Cup Course and the Smurfit Course. The beautiful estate provides a combination of difficult golf and elegant facilities.

Waterville Golf Links (County Kerry): Located on the Ring of Kerry, Waterville is a traditional links course famed for its tough design and spectacular vistas of the Atlantic. Golfers maneuver across dunes and enjoy a coastal golfing experience.

Adare Manor Golf Club (County Limerick): Set inside the grounds of the opulent Adare Manor, this championship course received a substantial makeover by Tom Fazio. The course incorporates parkland and riverbank aspects, delivering a demanding but scenic round.

County Sligo Golf Club (County Sligo): Nestled between Benbulben Mountain and the Atlantic, County Sligo Golf Club, known as Rosses Point, provides a links course with beautiful coastline vistas. The difficult course challenges golfers of all ability levels.

Druids Glen Golf Resort (County Wicklow): Often referred to as the "Augusta of Europe," Druids Glen is a parkland course surrounded by lush greenery and water features. The tough course and groomed grounds make it a favorite option for golf fans.

Whether you're a seasoned golfer seeking championship challenges or a casual player hoping to enjoy picturesque rounds, Ireland's golf courses give a broad variety of experiences. From historic links courses to lush parklands, these courses reflect the country's natural beauty and provide a golfing trip like no other.

Water Activities

Ireland's large coastline, lakes, and rivers provide a wealth of water-based activities for anyone seeking aquatic experiences. Whether you're into sailing, kayaking, or just exploring picturesque rivers, Ireland provides something for any water lover. Dive into the possibilities with these aquatic activities:

Sailing along the Wild Atlantic Way: The Wild Atlantic Way, spanning along Ireland's western coast, offers a spectacular setting for sailing. Charter a boat or join a sailing excursion to discover coastal cliffs, islands, and stunning bays.

Kayaking on Lough Corrib (County Galway): Lough Corrib, one of Ireland's biggest lakes, provides great kayaking options. Paddle across quiet waterways, discover secret coves, and enjoy views of ancient monuments such as Ashford Castle.

Surfing at Lahinch (County Clare): Lahinch, on the west coast, is a popular surfing area with regular waves. Whether you're a novice or an expert surfer, the Atlantic waves give a thrilling and stimulating surfing experience.

Canoeing on the River Boyne (County Meath): The River Boyne, steeped in history and surrounded by stunning surroundings, is suitable for a leisurely canoe excursion. Explore historic sites like the Bru na Boinne UNESCO World Heritage complex during your tour.

Diving in the Skellig Islands (County Kerry): For a unique underwater experience, try diving near the Skellig Islands. Explore the varied marine life, sea caves, and underwater rock formations around these historic islands.

Stand-Up Paddleboarding at Killarney (County Kerry): Paddleboard on the tranquil lakes of Killarney National Park for a relaxing water excursion. Take in the stunning vistas of mountains and trees as you traverse the tranquil waters.

Sea Kayaking at Clew Bay (County Mayo): Clew Bay, with its 365 islands, is a sea kayaker's delight. Paddle around the calm waters, finding secret coves and ancient sights like Clare Island, with its medieval monastery.

Coasteering on the Causeway Coast (County Antrim): Embrace the excitement of coasteering along the magnificent Causeway Coast. Jump, climb, and swim through sea caves and natural rock features while enjoying the harsh coastline environment.

Windsurfing at Brandon Bay (County Kerry): Brandon Bay, on the Dingle Peninsula, is famous for its constant winds, making it a perfect spot for windsurfing. Experience the excitement of catching the wind and surfing the waves.

River Rafting on the River Shannon (Multiple Counties): The River Shannon, Ireland's longest river, provides chances for river rafting. Navigate the rapids and enjoy the picturesque splendor as you float through the heart of the nation.

Fishing in Connemara (County Galway): Connemara, with its lakes and rivers, is a sanctuary for fishers. Try your hand at fly fishing or angling for salmon and trout in the pristine waterways of this lovely location.

Whale viewing in West Cork: West Cork is a hotspot for whale viewing, notably in sites like Baltimore and Clonakilty. Join a boat excursion to observe spectacular marine life, including dolphins, seals, and potentially even whales.

Kitesurfing at Achill Island (County Mayo): Achill Island provides outstanding conditions for kitesurfing. With its large beaches and strong Atlantic winds, it's a perfect site for both beginners and expert kitesurfers.

Canyoning in Connemara (County Galway): Explore Connemara's harsh terrain via canyoning. Descend waterfalls, swim in natural pools, and visit the magnificent Connemara National Park.

Sail on Lough Erne (County Fermanagh): Experience the peacefulness of Lough Erne with a leisurely sail. Explore the interconnecting lakes and canals, passing by historic landmarks, and enjoying the calm surroundings.

Whether you're seeking adrenaline-pumping sports or a quiet day on the water, Ireland's numerous waterways offer to all tastes. Dive into these aquatic experiences and explore the beauty that lies throughout the shores, lakes, and rivers of the Emerald Isle.

Cycling Routes

Ireland's various landscapes offer a fantastic background for bicycle lovers. From seaside roads to mountain trails, cycling routes are catering to all ability levels. Here are some gorgeous bike routes to visit in Ireland:

Great Western Greenway (County Mayo): Enjoy a gorgeous ride along the Great Western Greenway, a traffic-free cycling trail that extends from Westport to Achill Island. Pass through picturesque towns, enjoy Clew Bay, and absorb the splendor of Ireland's west coast.

Ring of Kerry (County Kerry): The Ring of Kerry provides a traditional cycling route with beautiful views of coastal cliffs, mountains, and lakes. Starting and concluding in Killarney, this circuit takes you via Killorglin, Glenbeigh, Cahersiveen, Waterville, Sneem, and Kenmare.

Waterford Greenway (County Waterford): The Waterford Greenway is a lovely bicycle track created on a disused railway line. Cycle from Waterford to Dungarvan, traveling through picturesque towns, viaducts, and the magnificent Copper Coast Geopark.

The Burren (County Clare): Explore the beautiful limestone terrain of the Burren on two wheels. The journey takes you across the lunar-like landscape, past historic ruins like Poulnabrone Dolmen, and affording spectacular views of the Atlantic.

Dingle Peninsula (County Kerry): Cycle the Dingle Peninsula, seeing the rugged beauty of Ireland's west coast. Enjoy breathtaking views of the Atlantic, see ancient places like Dunquin Pier, and appreciate the rich culture of Dingle Town.

The Wild Atlantic Way - Donegal Section (County Donegal): The Donegal stretch of the Wild Atlantic Way provides a hard and rewarding cycling adventure. Ride along the coastline, passing through rural landscapes, small settlements, and the gorgeous Glenveagh National Park.

The Blueway - Lough Derg (Counties Clare, Galway, Tipperary): Cycle around the beaches of Lough Derg, part of Ireland's Blueway network. This path includes stunning views of the lake, attractive towns, and the opportunity to discover the local history and culture.

The Copper Coast (County Waterford): The Copper Coast Geopark is not just a UNESCO Global Geopark but also a superb cycling destination. Follow the coastal roads and take in the spectacular vistas of cliffs, coves, and ancient mining sites.

The Aran Islands (County Galway): Explore the Aran Islands by bike, immersing yourself in the rich cultural history and breathtaking scenery. Cycle through Inishmore, Inishmaan, and Inisheer, exploring historic forts, stone walls, and stunning coastline panoramas.

Slea Head Drive (County Kerry): Slea Head Drive provides a demanding and rewarding cycling route across the Dingle Peninsula. Marvel at the renowned Blasket Islands, old beehive houses, and the majestic cliffs of Dunmore Head.

The Royal Canal Greenway (Multiple Counties): The Royal Canal Greenway is a bicycle path that follows the ancient Royal Canal, from Dublin to Longford. Enjoy the serene canal vistas, travel through attractive villages, and experience the rich history along the route.

The Boyne Valley Cycle Route (Counties Meath, Louth): Cycle through the ancient Boyne Valley, past monuments including the Hill of Tara and Newgrange. This journey blends picturesque landscapes with archaeological treasures and gives an insight into Ireland's ancient history.

The Giant's Causeway Coastal Route (County Antrim): Experience the magnificent beauty of Northern Ireland on the Giant's Causeway Coastal Route. Cycle around the Causeway Coast, past attractions including Carrick-a-Rede Rope Bridge and the famed Giant's Causeway.

The Dublin Bay Cycle Path (County Dublin): Enjoy a leisurely pedal along the Dublin Bay pedal Path, which extends from Sutton to Sandycove. Take in views of Dublin Bay, cruise through beach communities, and tour the famous Martello Towers.

The Great Southern Trail (Counties Limerick, Kerry): The Great Southern Trail follows a historic railway line, giving a pleasant cycling path through the gorgeous landscapes between Limerick and Kerry. Pass through gorgeous towns and villages, and experience the calm of rural Ireland.

Whether you're an ardent cyclist seeking demanding routes or a leisurely rider hoping to take in the beauty, Ireland's cycling routes appeal to all interests. Grab your bike, grab your helmet, and peddle around the stunning landscapes of the Emerald Isle.

Chapter Eight: Unique Experiences

Traditional Irish Music

Ireland's musical legacy is profoundly established in tradition, with a rich tapestry of songs and melodies that convey tales of love, grief, and history. Explore the enchanting world of traditional Irish music and immerse yourself in the melodies that resound through the heart of the Emerald Isle:

Session at an Irish bar: One of the most genuine ways to enjoy traditional Irish music is by joining a session in a local bar. Musicians assemble to perform melodies on instruments like the violin, tin whistle, bodhrán (drum), and accordion. The casual setting offers an intimate and energetic environment.

Celtic Music Festivals: Attend one of Ireland's numerous Celtic music festivals, where famous performers and new talent join together to celebrate the country's musical legacy. The Ennis Trad Festival and Willie Clancy Summer School in County Clare are famous for their dynamic programs and courses.

Riverdance or Irish Dance concerts: While not entirely centered on music, Riverdance and other Irish dance concerts typically contain live traditional music performances. The mix of complex footwork and vibrant rhythms provides a fascinating sight that has won worldwide praise.

Doolin Music House (County Clare): Visit the house of famous violinist Christy Barry in Doolin for an intimate and personal traditional music experience. The Doolin Music House provides visitors the chance to hear live performances in a pleasant environment while learning about the history of Irish music.

Visit Trad Music Schools: Enroll in a traditional music school to receive hands-on experience with Irish instruments and traditions. Many institutions offer short courses or seminars where you may learn to play the tin whistle, violin, or bodhrán, supervised by professional teachers.

Fleadh Cheoil na hÉireann: Join the thrill of Fleadh Cheoil, the greatest yearly festival of Irish song, dancing, and culture. The festival travels to new sites each year, presenting contests, concerts, and street sessions. It's a dynamic and engaging experience for music aficionados.

Celtic Connections (Glasgow, Scotland): While not in Ireland, the Celtic Connections event in Glasgow, Scotland, invites Irish performers and emphasizes the interconnectivity of Celtic traditions. It's a terrific chance to enjoy a varied selection of Celtic music genres.

Traditional Music Museums: Explore museums devoted to traditional Irish music, such as the Clare Heritage and Genealogical Centre. These organizations give insights into the history of Irish music, incorporating displays, instruments, and recordings.

Irish Folk Music Tours: Join a folk music tour that takes you across the heartlands of traditional Irish music. These excursions generally involve trips to historic music venues, sessions in local pubs, and meetings with professional musicians who share their skills.

Whether you're tapping your foot to a lively reel in a bar, visiting a music festival, or learning to play a traditional instrument, immersing yourself in the world of Irish music promises a soul-stirring experience that connects with the essence of the Emerald Isle.

Pub Culture

Ireland's pub culture is a vital aspect of the nation's character, giving more than simply a venue to sip a pint. It's a social institution where companionship, storytelling, and live music come together. Dive into the heart of Irish bar culture with these insights:

Warm Hospitality: Irish pubs are famous for their inviting environment. Whether you're a native or a guest, anticipate welcoming faces and a feeling of belonging. The pub is a community area where strangers become friends over shared tales and laughs.

Live Music Sessions: Music is the lifeblood of Irish pubs. Many places hold live music sessions, showcasing traditional Irish melodies, folk songs, and occasionally even spontaneous performances. The violin, tin whistle, bodhrán, and guitar commonly complement the energetic mood.

Traditional Irish Pubs: Seek out the charm of traditional Irish pubs with their warm interiors, wooden furniture, and sometimes centuries-old architecture. Places like The Temple Bar in Dublin, Tigh Neachtain in Galway, and The Crown Liquor Saloon in Belfast provide a genuine pub atmosphere.

Pouring the Perfect Pint: Guinness, Ireland's famed stout, is a fixture in pubs throughout the nation. Witness the art of pouring the perfect pint, a talent that entails a precise two-part pour and settling time, producing the creamy head that marks a well-poured Guinness.

Snug sections and Nooks: Many Irish pubs offer snug sections or nooks—semi-private rooms where guests may enjoy a calmer drink or a discussion away from the main bar area. These snug spaces contribute to the personal and community atmosphere of the tavern.

Pub Grub & Comfort cuisine: Pubs in Ireland generally provide substantial comfort cuisine to complement your beverages. From traditional Irish stew and fish & chips to innovative variations on classic meals, the pub menu caters to a range of preferences.

Storytelling culture: Pubs are a center for storytelling, and Ireland has a long oral culture. Expect to hear stories of local folklore, historical events, and hilarious anecdotes. The bar is a place where tales are exchanged and maintained.

Themed Pub Nights: Some pubs host themed nights, celebrating everything from traditional Irish music to quiz nights and themed costume parties. These events lend a dynamic flavor to the bar scene, producing an ever-changing and stimulating ambiance.

Community Hubs: Pubs typically operate as community hubs, hosting events, fundraisers, and gatherings. From local sports screens to charitable efforts, the bar plays a crucial role in uniting individuals within an area.

Prolonged Opening Hours: In many Irish towns and cities, pubs have prolonged opening hours compared to certain other nations. This allows for a more calm and slower pace, enabling clients to absorb the occasion.

To genuinely understand Irish pub culture, take your time, startup discussions with locals, and let the ambiance absorb you. Whether you're enjoying a quiet pint by the fireplace or stomping your feet to live music, the pub is where the essence of Ireland comes alive.

Festivals and Events

Ireland's festival calendar is a rich tapestry of cultural, musical, and historical events that attract residents and tourists alike. From ancient festivities to contemporary gatherings, these festivals provide a variety of experiences throughout the year:

St. Patrick's Day (Nationwide): Celebrated on March 17th, St. Patrick's Day is a worldwide event, but experiencing it in Ireland is unrivaled. Cities like Dublin, Cork, and Galway explode with parades, music, and a sea of green as the country commemorates its patron saint.

Galway International Arts Festival (Galway): Held in July, this diverse arts event turns Galway into a cultural hotspot. Expect world-class concerts, visual arts, street spectacles, and a celebratory atmosphere that brings the city to life.

Electric Picnic (County Laois): As one of Ireland's best music events, Electric Picnic takes place on Stradbally Estate every September. Boasting a broad roster of international and local bands, it's a must-attend event for music aficionados.

Dublin Horse Show (Dublin): August brings the Dublin Horse Show, a famous equestrian event hosted at the RDS Arena. Showcasing top-class show jumping, dressage, and entertainment, it's a fantastic event for horse enthusiasts.

Bloomsday (Dublin): Celebrate James Joyce's masterwork "Ulysses" on June 16th on Bloomsday. Events include readings, plays, and walking tours that immerse people in the setting of the book, situated in Dublin.

Fleadh Cheoil na hÉireann (Various sites): The biggest traditional Irish music event, Fleadh Cheoil travels to various sites each. Attend contests, performances, and seminars highlighting the finest of Irish traditional music, dancing, and culture.

Cork Jazz Festival (Cork): October sees the Cork Jazz Festival, a colorful celebration of jazz music. The event takes over the city's streets, taverns, and venues, presenting performances by local and worldwide jazz performers.

All-Ireland Hurling and Football Finals (Dublin): Experience the passion of Gaelic sports during the All-Ireland Hurling and Football Finals hosted at Croke Park in September. These tournaments represent the finale of the GAA (Gaelic Athletic Association) season, bringing people from around the country.

Listowel Writers' Week (County Kerry): Literary aficionados gather to Listowel in May for Writers' Week, a celebration of Irish and worldwide literature. The event comprises readings, seminars, and talks with prominent writers.

Dingle Cinema Festival (County Kerry): For cinema connoisseurs, the Dingle Film Festival in March shows a broad range of Irish and foreign films. The gorgeous environment adds to the beauty of this movie experience.

Kilkenny Arts Festival (County Kilkenny): Held in August, the Kilkenny Arts Festival mixes classical music, visual arts, and drama in the medieval city of Kilkenny. The event draws artists and spectators from throughout the globe.

Cruinniú na nÓg (Nationwide): Aimed at young people, Cruinniú na nÓg is a National Day of Creativity celebrated in June. Communities around Ireland hold events and activities, enabling children and teens to use their creative skills.

Planning your vacation around these festivals and events gives an immersive and dynamic experience, enabling you to observe the unique cultural fabric of Ireland throughout the year.

Gaelic Games

Gaelic sports, profoundly steeped in Ireland's cultural fabric, constitute a distinctive and intense athletic history. These historic Irish sports, controlled by the Gaelic Athletic Association (GAA), enthrall both participants and spectators. Immerse yourself in the thrilling world of Gaelic games:

Hurling: Widely recognized as one of the quickest and oldest field games in the world, hurling mixes skill, speed, and toughness. Players use a wooden stick, called a hurley, to strike a tiny ball (sliotar) between the other team's goalposts. The All-Ireland Hurling Championship, contested annually, is a major event in Irish sports.

Gaelic Football: Gaelic football is a dynamic sport that incorporates aspects of soccer and rugby. Teams of 15 players seek to score points by kicking or hitting the ball into the other team's goal or over the crossbar. The All-Ireland Football Championship is a highlight of the Gaelic football calendar.

Camogie: Camogie is the female equivalent of hurling, played with the same rules and equipment. It exhibits the same high-paced action and skill, with enthusiastic players engaged in intense contests. The All-Ireland Camogie Championship is a prominent championship for female players.

Ladies' Gaelic Football: Ladies' Gaelic football parallels its male counterpart but has established its own identity and fanbase. The sport has witnessed a substantial increase in popularity, with women's teams participating at local, national, and international levels.

Handball: Gaelic handball is a unique sport played in alleys with a tiny, hard ball. Players use their hands to hit the ball against a wall, hoping to make it difficult for their opponent to return. The sport includes variants, including one-wall and four-wall handball.

Rounders: A classic Irish bat-and-ball game, rounders involve teams taking turns hitting and fielding. It bears similarities with baseball and softball and is played in both official and casual settings.

Gaelic Athletic Association (GAA) Club sports: Beyond the county and national tournaments, local GAA clubs are the heart of Gaelic sports. Joining a local club gives a chance to actively engage in these activities, developing a feeling of community and friendship.

Croke Park Stadium (Dublin): Croke Park, situated in Dublin, is the headquarters of the GAA and the famous location for major Gaelic sports events. Attending a match at Croke Park enables you to feel the passion and intensity of these sports in a historic venue.

Gaelic sports Experience for tourists: Many GAA clubs allow tourists to experience Gaelic sports firsthand. Participate in hurling or Gaelic football seminars, where expert teachers share insights into the skills and strategies involved.

Comórtas Peile na Gaeltachta (Gaelic Football event in Gaeltacht communities): This yearly event in Gaeltacht regions displays the unique cultural and sports history of these Irish-speaking communities. Teams from Gaeltacht areas engage in Gaelic football, celebrating both language and sport.

Gaelic games are more than simply sports in Ireland; they symbolize a link to tradition, community, and the eternal spirit of competitiveness. Whether you're watching a match at Croke Park or trying your hand at hurling in a small club, embracing Gaelic sports gives a fascinating insight into Ireland's dynamic athletic culture.

Chapter Nine: Culinary Delights

Traditional Irish Cuisine

Ireland's culinary landscape is steeped in tradition, reflecting the country's rich history and rural origins. A vacation to Ireland is incomplete without indulging in the rich and healthy tastes of traditional Irish food. Here's a guide to the gastronomic pleasures that await you:

Irish Stew: Begin your gourmet excursion with the renowned Irish stew. This soul-warming recipe comprises soft slices of lamb or beef, combined with potatoes, carrots, and onions. Slow-cooked to perfection, it epitomizes the spirit of Irish comfort cuisine.

Boxty: Experience the diversity of Irish cuisine with Boxty, a classic potato pancake. Made with grated potatoes, flour, and buttermilk, boxty may be served as a side dish or filled with other toppings. Its crisp surface and soft inside make it a pleasant treat.

Coddle: Dive into Dublin's culinary legacy with coddle, a hearty stew comprising sausages, bacon, potatoes, and onions. This delectable recipe is a testimony to Irish home cuisine, emphasizing the simplicity and richness of local ingredients.

Colcannon: Elevate your dining experience with colcannon, a combination of creamy mashed potatoes and finely chopped kale or cabbage. Infused with the tastes of spring onions and butter, this side dish is a fantastic companion to numerous main dishes.

Irish Soda Bread: Savor the spirit of Irish baking with soda bread. Made with a mixture of flour, baking soda, buttermilk, and salt, this bread is a mainstay in Irish families. Pair it with butter for a simple but delightful flavor of traditional Irish cooking.

Barmbrack: Indulge your sweet taste with barmbrack, a spiced fruitcake that has a unique place in Irish tradition, especially around Halloween. Sliced and served with a liberal spread of butter, this delicacy delivers a delicious combination of tastes.

Irish Coffee: Conclude your gastronomic adventure with the world-famous Irish coffee. A harmonious blend of hot coffee, Irish whiskey, and a crown of cream, this beverage provides a comforting and invigorating finale to your Irish dining experience.

As you tour the picturesque streets of Ireland, visit local pubs and restaurants to enjoy the true flavors of these classic delicacies. Many places take pleasure in procuring fresh, local ingredients, ensuring that every taste is a celebration of Ireland's culinary history. Prepare your taste buds for a voyage into the heart and soul of Irish cuisine, where each dish offers a narrative of history, kindness, and hospitality.

Pubs and Restaurants

Exploring the thriving culinary scene in Ireland requires immersing yourself in the comfortable environment of traditional pubs and relishing wonderful meals at lovely eateries. Here's a guide to several prominent establishments that exemplify the spirit of Irish hospitality:

The Brazen Head (Dublin): Ireland's oldest bar, The Brazen Head, radiates character and history. Nestled in the center of Dublin, this historic business provides a pleasant environment, live music, and a cuisine comprising typical Irish specialties. It's a must-visit for a real pub experience.

The Quays (Galway): Located along the River Corrib, The Quays in Galway is noted for its vibrant atmosphere and traditional Irish music. Enjoy a pint of Guinness combined with substantial pub foods, like crab chowder and Irish lamb stew.

Bunratty Castle Medieval Banquet (County Clare): Immerse yourself in medieval eating at the Bunratty Castle banquet. Experience a feast fit for a king or queen, replete with traditional entertainment in a historic setting. It's a unique gastronomic voyage back in time.

Chapter One (Dublin): For a more sophisticated dining experience, Chapter One in Dublin provides modern Irish cuisine with an emphasis on locally produced ingredients. The exquisite environment and expertly made meals make it a favorite for those wanting a taste of contemporary Irish cuisine.

Fishy Fishy (Kinsale): Explore the seafood pleasures of Ireland at Fishy Fishy in Kinsale. With a cuisine featuring fresh fish from the Atlantic, this restaurant gives a seaside dining experience. The picturesque village contributes to the overall attractiveness of this gastronomic wonder.

The Porterhouse Brewing Company (Various Locations): If you're a beer fan, The Porterhouse Brewing Company is a must-visit. With outlets in Dublin, Bray, and London, this microbrewery provides a varied assortment of craft beers, coupled with a cuisine comprising pub classics with a contemporary twist.

Farmgate Café (Cork): Situated in the English Market, Farmgate Café in Cork highlights local products and traditional Irish cuisine. Enjoy a farm-to-table experience with meals that represent the finest of Cork's culinary tradition.

The Crown Liquor Saloon (Belfast): Step inside a Victorian-era masterpiece at The Crown Liquor Saloon in Belfast. Known for its magnificent décor and historic charm, this pub provides a broad range of drinks and cuisine including substantial Irish specialties.

Whether you're seeking the vibrant atmosphere of a traditional pub or the culinary expertise of a top-tier restaurant, Ireland's eating scene appeals to every palette.

From ancient pubs with centuries-old history to contemporary venues pushing culinary limits, your tour through Irish pubs and restaurants offers a memorable gourmet experience.

Food Festivals

Ireland's rich culinary traditions are on full display during its colorful food festivals when residents and tourists join together to enjoy the many tastes and ingredients that make Irish cuisine special. Immerse yourself in the pleasures of these food-centric events:

Galway International Oyster & Seafood Festival (Galway): Held annually in September, this world-renowned event displays Galway's seaside abundance. Indulge in freshly shucked oysters, seafood specialties, and a vibrant environment including live music and contests.

Dingle Food event (County Kerry): Set against the picturesque background of Dingle Peninsula, this event, normally held in October, promotes the finest of local products. Enjoy handmade cheeses, fresh fish, and traditional Irish meals while feeling the warmth of Dingle's hospitality.

Taste of Dublin (Dublin): Taking place in the heart of Dublin, this event is a gastronomic feast showcasing the city's greatest restaurants and chefs. Visitors may taste gourmet delicacies, witness culinary demos, and experience the varied flavors that Dublin's food sector has to offer.

Burren Slow Food event (County Clare): Celebrating the Slow Food movement, this event in Lisdoonvarna focuses on local, sustainable, and high-quality cuisine. Experience a weekend of tastings, seminars, and demonstrations amongst the beautiful limestone environment of the Burren.

Savour Kilkenny (County Kilkenny): Held in October, Savour Kilkenny is a food and drink event that brings together local chefs, producers, and food aficionados. Enjoy a range of culinary activities, from food markets to cookery demos, in the picturesque backdrop of Kilkenny.

Waterford Harvest celebration (Waterford): This September celebration in Waterford commemorates the region's gastronomic history. With a broad program featuring a farmer's market, food trails, and a family-friendly setting, it's a fantastic chance to discover Waterford's culinary scene.

Drogheda culinary and marine event (County Louth): Combining culinary and marine traditions, this event in Drogheda shows the best of both cultures. Enjoy seafood sampling, cookery demonstrations, and maritime-themed games in a colorful and family-friendly setting.

Glenarm Fish Festival (County Antrim): Celebrate Northern Ireland's culinary history with an emphasis on Glenarm's famed fish. The event comprises tastings, culinary demos, and activities for all ages, delivering a great experience in a lovely seaside environment.

Attending these food festivals gives a unique chance to engage with local farmers, chefs, and other food aficionados. It's an opportunity to sample the genuine flavors of Ireland, appreciate the attention to excellent ingredients, and enjoy the convivial environment that makes Irish food festivals distinctive.

Chapter Ten: Essential Travel Information

Language and Communication

Official Languages: Ireland has two official languages: English and Irish (Gaeilge). While English is the major language spoken, Irish is also taught in schools and is spoken in select Gaeltacht communities.

English Dialect: The English spoken in Ireland has distinct accents and idioms. Don't be shocked if you encounter terminology or phrases that vary from those in other English-speaking nations.

Common Phrases in Irish:

While English is frequently used, knowing a few words in Irish (Gaeilge) might be appreciated:

Hello: Dia dhuit (pronounced: dee-ah wit)

Thank you: Go raibh maith agat (pronounced: goh roh my gut)

Goodbye: Slán (pronounced: lawn)

Yes: Tá (pronounced: taw)

No: Níl (pronounced: Neel)

Politeness and Friendliness: Irish people are noted for their warmth and civility. It's customary to engage in small chat and employ polite language in social situations.

Public Transportation Announcements: In metropolitan areas and public transit, announcements and signage are often in both English and Irish. Train and bus services frequently give information in both languages.

Emergency Services: In case of emergencies, the official language for communication with emergency services is English. The phone number for emergency assistance is 112 or 999. 7. Language in Gaeltacht Areas:

Some locations in Ireland, known as Gaeltacht regions, have a greater proportion of Irish speakers. While English is still generally known, you may hear more Irish spoken in certain regions.

Tipping Etiquette: Tipping is traditional in Ireland. In restaurants, it is typical to leave a tip of roughly 10-15% of the bill if service is not included.

Wi-Fi and Internet: Wi-Fi is generally offered in metropolitan areas, hotels, cafés, and public places. If you require internet connectivity on the fly, consider buying a local SIM card or utilizing public Wi-Fi hotspots.

Time Zone: Ireland runs on Greenwich Mean Time (GMT) in the winter and Irish Standard Time (IST), which is GMT+1, in the summer months.

Cultural Sensitivity: Be conscious of cultural sensitivities, and approach talks on delicate themes, such as politics or religion, with respect. Irish people are typically cordial, and a warm and open manner is valued.

Understanding the linguistic and cultural nuances will enhance your travel experience in Ireland. Whether conversing in English or trying a few sentences in Irish, the friendly inhabitants will certainly appreciate your attempts to engage with the local culture.

Health and Safety Tips

Travel Insurance: Ensure you have adequate travel insurance that covers medical expenditures, emergency evacuation, and unexpected trip cancellations.

Emergency Services: The emergency services number in Ireland is 112 or 999. Keep this number accessible for any needed help.

Health Precautions: No special vaccines are necessary for visiting Ireland, however, it's best to be up-to-date on standard immunizations. Carry any essential prescription drugs and a basic first aid kit.

Healthcare System: Ireland has a public healthcare system, and EU nationals possessing a European Health Insurance Card (EHIC) are eligible for emergency services. Non-EU citizens should have adequate travel insurance.

Weather Preparedness: Ireland's weather may be unpredictable. Pack layers, waterproof clothes, and sturdy shoes. Check the weather forecast periodically, particularly if planning outside activities.

Road Safety: If you intend to drive, educate yourself about local traffic restrictions. Drive on the left side of the road. Ensure everyone in the car wears seatbelts, and avoid driving under the influence of alcohol.

Currency and Card Safety: Keep your valuables safe, and be careful with your stuff in busy locations. Notify your bank about your trip dates to prevent complications with card transactions.

Water Safety: While tap water is safe to drink in Ireland, if you're trekking or camping, it's suggested to take a reusable water bottle. Be careful near cliffs and bodies of water, particularly during poor weather conditions.

Outdoor Adventure Safety: If indulging in outdoor activities, such as hiking or visiting coastal regions, be alert of your surroundings. Follow safety requirements and advise someone of your intentions, particularly in isolated places.

COVID-19 Guidelines: Stay updated about the newest COVID-19 standards and limitations. Adhere to public health precautions, including mask-wearing and social separation, as suggested by local authorities.

Respect Local Customs: Be aware of and respect local traditions and cultural standards. Ireland is typically a safe destination, but it's vital to apply the same care you would in any strange country.

Insect Protection: In rural settings, particularly during warmer months, consider applying insect repellent to guard against ticks and midges.

Emergency Contacts: Keep a list of vital contacts, including the contact details of your country's embassy or consulate in Ireland, in case of crises.

Sun Protection: Even on gloomy days, UV radiation may be intense. Use sunscreen, wear sunglasses, and cover up to protect your skin.

Local Emergency Numbers: Familiarize yourself with local emergency numbers and contacts, including those of neighboring hospitals and clinics.

By adopting some health and safety measures, you may ensure a smooth and pleasurable travel in Ireland. Stay educated, practice common sense, and appreciate the pleasant and inviting attitude of this lovely nation.

Customs and Etiquette

Greetings: Irish people are noted for their kindness. When meeting someone, a simple "hello" or "hi" is sufficient. A strong handshake is a customary greeting, and keeping eye contact displays sincerity.

Politeness and Courtesy: Politeness is highly prized in Irish society. Use "please" and "thank you" freely, and respect social graces. Holding doors open for others and providing aid when required are appreciated gestures.

Personal Space: Irish people often cherish personal space. While interactions are cordial, keep a comfortable distance while conversing with others.

Punctuality: Punctuality is vital in professional contexts. Arrive on time for appointments and meetings. In social circumstances, being a bit late is often acceptable.

Communication Style: Irish communication is frequently oblique, with individuals employing humor and subtle clues. It's normal to engage in small chat, so be prepared for polite interactions with locals.

Pub Etiquette: In pubs, wait to be served at your table or the bar. It's normal to give a cordial welcome or nod while entering. If someone gives you a drink, it's courteous to reciprocate.

Gift-Giving: If invited to someone's house, it's usual to offer a little gift, such as flowers, chocolates, or a bottle of wine. A thank-you letter or a follow-up communication is welcomed.

Dining Etiquette: Wait for the host to start the dinner before you begin eating. It's polite to eat everything on your plate, and it's usual to say "please" when asking for something and "thank you" after getting it.

Respect for Traditions: Irish people take pride in their cultural history. Show respect for traditions, particularly during festivals or religious events. Learn a few words in Irish (Gaeilge) to exhibit cultural respect.

Dress Code: Dress conservatively while visiting religious locations. In informal contexts, smart-casual clothes are often adequate. Check the dress code if you want to attend a more formal event.

Acknowledge Differences: Ireland is noted for its geographical distinctions and diverse local cultures. Acknowledge and respect the variety within the nation.

Conversational Topics: Engage in talks about sports, literature, and culture. Avoid discussing delicate issues like politics and religion until requested to do so.

Be Hospitable: Irish hospitality is famous. If you're invited to someone's house, show thanks and participate in the social element of the visit. Offer to assist with duties after a meal.

Embrace the Local Customs: Participate in local customs and traditions, particularly during festivals and celebrations. This displays your interest in and admiration for Irish culture.

By being attentive to these traditions and etiquette suggestions, you may enrich your experience in Ireland and connect more intimately with the warm and hospitable Irish people.

Eco-Friendly Practices

Ireland is increasingly focusing on sustainable and eco-friendly efforts. As a responsible visitor, here are ways to help the country's environmental efforts:

Sustainable Accommodation: Choose eco-friendly lodgings accredited by groups like Green Hospitality Ireland. These institutions promote energy efficiency, waste reduction, and conservation techniques.

Public Transportation: Opt for public transit, such as trains and buses, which have reduced carbon footprints compared to private vehicle rentals. Explore cities on foot or by bicycle to reduce your environmental effects.

Responsible Hiking and Outdoor Activities: Follow authorized trails and walkways to safeguard natural environments. Adhere to the principles of "Leave No Trace" by properly disposing of waste and respecting wildlife.

Eco-Friendly Tours: Participate in eco-friendly excursions that stress environmental protection and education. Consider excursions that concentrate on sustainable techniques and ethical animal watching.

Reduce Plastic Usage: Carry a reusable water bottle to reduce single-use plastics. Refill stations are found in numerous areas. Bring a reusable bag while shopping to decrease plastic waste.

Support Local and Sustainable Products: Purchase locally created items and support companies that promote sustainability. Look for eco-friendly certificates on items, demonstrating conformity to environmental standards.

Responsible Wildlife Tourism: If participating in wildlife tourism, consider operators dedicated to ethical procedures. Avoid actions that entail animal exploitation or disturbance of natural ecosystems.

Energy Conservation: Conserve energy by turning off lights and devices when not in use. Choose lodgings that employ energy-efficient strategies.

Waste Reduction: Practice waste minimization by recycling and properly disposing of garbage. Be informed of local recycling requirements and engage in community clean-up programs.

Environmental Education: Learn about local ecosystems, conservation activities, and environmental problems. Engaging with local environmental projects or attending nature-oriented educational programs leads to awareness and support.

Green Events & Festivals: Attend events and festivals that stress sustainability. Many events in Ireland now feature eco-friendly initiatives, such as trash reduction and recycling programs.

Sustainable Dining: Choose restaurants that emphasize locally produced, organic, and sustainable food alternatives. Support enterprises that promote ethical agricultural and fishing techniques.

Stay on Designated Paths: When touring natural reserves, parks, and picturesque locations, stick to approved trails to prevent hurting vulnerable ecosystems.

Eco-Friendly Transportation: If renting a vehicle, investigate electric or hybrid choices. Some rental firms in Ireland provide eco-friendly car alternatives.

Offset Your Carbon Footprint: Consider carbon offset schemes to pay for your travel-related emissions. Many organizations provide possibilities to invest in environmental initiatives.

By implementing these eco-friendly habits into your holiday schedule, you contribute to Ireland's sustainable efforts and help preserve the country's natural beauty for future generations.

Local Community Engagement

Connecting with local communities is a meaningful approach to improve your trip experience in Ireland. Here are methods to interact with and help the local communities you encounter:

Attend Local Events and Festivals: Participate in local events, festivals, and cultural festivities. This not only offers you a genuine experience but also helps the local economy and shows the community's traditions.

Visit Farmers' Markets: Explore farmers' markets where local growers and craftspeople present their goods. Purchasing locally-produced items help directly to the livelihoods of community people.

Stay at Locally-Owned Accommodations: Choose lodgings that are locally owned, such as boutique hotels, bed & breakfasts, or guesthouses. This guarantees that a considerable amount of your expenditure goes directly to the community.

Dine in Local Restaurants: Opt for locally-owned restaurants and cafes that highlight locally-produced food. Engage with the staff and learn about the culinary traditions of the region.

Take Guided Tours with Locals: Consider guided tours offered by local inhabitants who may provide insights into the history, culture, and hidden jewels of their city. This supports local entrepreneurs and encourages cultural exchange.

Attend Workshops & Classes: Participate in workshops or seminars provided by local craftspeople or specialists. This might include traditional music lessons, culinary courses, or artisan workshops. Your involvement helps maintain traditional skills and knowledge.

Volunteer in the Community: Look for volunteer opportunities in local areas. This might be engaging in environmental campaigns, community development projects, or supporting local charities. Volunteering builds a stronger connection with the community.

Support Local Artisans: Purchase handcrafted items and gifts directly from local craftsmen and artists. This not only ensures the authenticity of your purchases but also supports the livelihoods of talented individuals.

Learn About Local History and Traditions: Engage with locals to learn about the history and customs of the place. Visit museums, heritage sites, and cultural centers to gain a deeper understanding of the community's roots.

Attend Local Sports Events: If there's a local sporting event going on, attend and cheer for the home team. This gives a chance to meet with people and experience the love for sports in the community.

Respect Local Customs: Familiarize yourself with and respect local customs and traditions. This involves learning social conventions, greetings, and any unique etiquette popular in the locality.

Participate in Community Festivities: If there's a community fair, procession, or other festivities going place, participate in the celebrations. These events frequently give a peek into the heart of the town and its inhabitants.

Support Community-Based Tourism programs: Look for community-based tourism programs that empower local populations. This might incorporate homestays, community-led tours, or other programs that directly engage the community in tourist operations.

Practice Responsible Tourism: Be careful of your environmental effects and implement sustainable and responsible travel practices. Respect local resources and help protect the natural beauty of the place.

Seek advice from Locals: Ask locals for advice on places to visit, eat, and explore. This not only delivers significant information but also creates great connections with community members.

By actively interacting with local communities, you contribute to sustainable tourism and develop important relationships with the people who call Ireland home. Your courteous and responsible attitude benefits both your travel experience and the well-being of the communities you visit.

Leave No Trace Principles

As you journey into Ireland's stunning landscapes, it's vital to adhere to the Leave No Trace guidelines to limit your influence on the environment. Follow these rules to protect the natural beauty and integrity of Ireland's outdoor spaces:

Plan and Prepare: Research and organize your vacation in advance. Be cognizant of legislation, weather conditions, and any possible environmental problems. Equip yourself with the correct gear for the activities you'll conduct.

Stick to Designated Trails: Stay on established trails to avoid trampling on fragile vegetation and disturbing wildlife. This helps protect the natural habitats and ensures that ecosystems remain intact.

Dispose of Waste Properly: Pack out all rubbish, including food leftovers and biodegradable garbage. Dispose of rubbish in approved containers or take it with you until you can properly dispose of it. Leave the environment as you found it.

Leave What You Find: Avoid plucking plants, damaging rocks, or removing any cultural or historical relics. Leave natural and cultural features as you encountered them for others to enjoy.

Minimize Campfire Impact: If campfires are authorized and essential, utilize existing fire rings or portable stoves. Keep fires small, and never leave them unattended. Ensure the fire is extinguished before leaving.

Respect Wildlife: Observe animals from a distance, using binoculars or a camera. Do not approach or feed animals, since it might disturb their normal habits and diets. Keep dogs on a leash and under control.

Be Considerate of Other Visitors: Keep noise levels down and respect the isolation of others. Yield the route to walkers, and be kind to other outdoor lovers. Avoid loud music and disrupting activities.

Camp Responsibly: Choose established campsites where possible, and camp at least 200 feet away from lakes and streams to preserve water sources. Follow Leave No Trace camping guidelines to minimize your influence.

Travel and Camp on Durable Surfaces: Stick to designated routes, trails, and campsites to reduce soil erosion and harm to plants. Avoid developing new paths or shortcuts.

Be Aware of Local Regulations: Familiarize oneself with and observe any special restrictions or recommendations imposed by municipal authorities, park management, or conservation groups. Adhering to these standards helps safeguard sensitive regions.

Leave Cultural Features Undisturbed: Avoid touching, leaning on, or disturbing cultural and historical features. Respect ancient sites, monuments, and constructions by avoiding modifying or vandalizing them.

Educate Yourself and Others: Continuously educate yourself on Leave No Trace principles and share this information with others. Encourage appropriate outdoor conduct and assist develop a culture of environmental care.

By adopting the Leave No Trace principles, you help to the preservation of Ireland's natural marvels, ensuring they stay pure and accessible for future generations of residents and tourists alike.

Printed in Great Britain
by Amazon

38767236R00096